NOTES FROM THE CHRISTIAN CIRCUS

by
Jack Barranger

THE BOOK TREE
San Diego, California

© 2015
Jack Barranger
All rights reserved

No part of this publication may be used or transmitted in any way without the expressed written consent of the publisher, except for short excerpts for use in reviews.

ISBN 978-1-58509-147-8

Cover layout by
Mike Sparrow

Interior layout & design
Eric Dobko

Published by
The Book Tree
P O Box 16476
San Diego, CA 92176
www.thebooktree.com

We provide fascinating and educational products to help awaken the public to new ideas and information that would not be available otherwise.
Call 1 (800) 700-8733 for our FREE BOOK TREE CATALOG.

CONTENTS

Foreword……………….......…..……………….………….…..5

1) The Horace Valley Prayer Contest……………..………..……7

2) Jesus Encounters the Growth Freaks………...……………..…13

3) Talking Christian Head Trip Blues……………..…………….25

4) Christianity on Five Dollars a Day...……………..….…..……..27

5) Television Relic 666……………………………….………….39

6) A Somewhat Modest Proposal..……………………………….45

7) The Big Game….......……………………………………..49

8) A Radical Christian Looks at Explo 72..………….…………59

9) From the Circus to the Arena...………………….....……..91

Appendix: Jakov Speaks on the Divine Imperative……………..111

FOREWORD

Someone once asked me, after he had read one of Jack Barranger's books on the pitiful condition of organized religion in modern society, "Is he trying to be funny or what?" My answer was "Or what." My nonplussed questioner blinked twice, nodded, then silently turned and walked away. So much for my attempt at humor.

But I thought about that moment as I was reading *Notes from the Christian Circus*. Not because I was chortling or guffawing, which I seldom do, but because I was reminded of Professor Scully's attempt, in 1902, to define a smile, as cited by Richard Usborne in his treatise on P. G. Wodehouse: "the drawing back and slight lifting of the corners of the mouth, which partially uncover the teeth; the curving of the naso-labial furrows ..."

Now that made me chortle and guffaw. Barranger, on the other hand, makes me experience a definite naso-labial furrow from time to time, and reading *Notes from the Christian Circus* was one of those times. It is not a "funny" book. In fact, it is a serious questioning of modern Christian practices and attitudes from the viewpoint of a former seminary student who had begun to notice the distinct difference between religion and true spirituality. However, it is filled with Barranger's usual biting wit and understated sarcasm when those are appropriate. And, quite frankly, the condition of Christianity today cries out for the kind of satiric wit and sarcasm that inevitably leads to the drawing back and slight lifting of the corners of the mouth.

Notes from the Christian Circus is a series of essays that were written in the early 1970's. Now, I know what you're thinking. "Nineteen-seventies! I wasn't even born then!" That is, of course, if you were born after 1980 and are under the impression that nothing of any significance happened in the world prior to then. And if you are a graduate of the California public school system, that is a distinct likelihood.

To be perfectly honest, however, I too wondered why anyone would be interested in the ancient history of pre-disco America. The answer can be found in a French proverb, which I am going to translate into English to prevent anyone reading this from getting a severe headache: The more things change, the more they stay the same. Our culture, our economy and especially our language have changed considerably. But we haven't. And Christianity hasn't either, for the most part. Aside from passages that contain such painful uses of the terms "where it's at" and "groovy," these essays could have been written yesterday.

That is particularly true of the essay A Radical Christian Looks at Explo 72. Me, I had never even heard of Explo 72 and had felt no gaping hole in my life because of that. I wondered, when I first began to read it, why anyone, anywhere would even care what Explo 72 was or what happened during it. But as I read, I began to realize that the date of its occurrence had no significance. This story is about people of all ages and all times who are struggling to find God, enlightenment, the meaning of life. The questions it deals with are timeless, the time is irrelevant.

After looking at fundamentalist zeal (The Horace Valley Prayer Contest), what Jesus would experience if he suddenly showed up in the San Fernando Valley (Jesus Encounters the Growth Freaks), materialism (Christianity on Five Dollars a Day), avarice (A Somewhat Modest Proposal), inter-religious competition (The Big Game), an imaginative news report of the fulfillment of The Great Commission (Television Relic 666), Barranger concludes with a look at what Christianity could be if it gave up some of its sacred cows, hitched up its collective pants, spit on its hands and got to work (From the Circus to the Arena).

Notes From the Christian Circus is an intellectual and spiritual smorgasbord. It is neither anti-Christian nor anti-religion. It is anti-stupidity and anti-hypocrisy. Barranger cares about our relationship with God and our relationship with truth, whatever that is, much more than he cares about our relationship to authoritarian groups or social organizations or entrenched dogmas.

As with any good smorgasbord, there is something for just about everyone. So line up and chow down. You will know if you are getting anything from reading this when you notice you have to stop once in a while and digest what you've read. And, of course, you will occasionally notice the curving of your naso-labial furrows.

—John Anthony Presser

1

The Horace Valley Prayer Contest

I have had what I consider to be one of the most amazing experiences of my life. Actually I'm glad to be alive because I barely escaped with my life. My wife and two kids were gone for the weekend and I was left in solitude. I became itchy and needed to do something. I decided that I would take a long drive and get away for the weekend. I had no destination in mind; I would just start driving and see where I ended up. I jumped in my car and started driving. It felt good being on the road. I barely noticed the small towns as I drove through them. However, in Horace Valley one sign caught my attention:

Horace Valley Prayer Contest

The sun was setting and I figured I needed a place to stay, so I pulled in at a motel. I asked the man behind the desk about the prayer contest.

"Oh, that's the biggest event of the year. Only happens once a year. People get up and pray out loud before a panel of judges. Whoever prays they give first, second and third place for the best three pray-ers. It's held in the high school gym. Why don't you go? Do you have anything better to do?"

I told him that I didn't, and he gave me directions to the gym.

I arrived and found about five hundred people brimming with anticipation. People, I eventually discovered, through a series of "pray-offs" before the main contest; the best people from the pray-offs got to pray at the main event.

The emcee approached the microphone.

"Our first prayer tonight will be Ed Gillespy. Ed placed third in last year's contest. But he has promised that he's going to rip off with a good one tonight. We just might have a winner here. Ed, get your butt up here and pray a good one."

Ed stepped up to the mike, cleared his throat, and began:

"Lord, we thank thee for thy bounteous blessings. We thank thee, and the glory shall be thine alone. Thou art the mighty one and we tremble before thee. Give us thy blessing so that we might go forth, and thou shalt be glorified. Let honor be thine, and let us stand before thee, and thou shalt be righteous and sanctified. In Jesus's name we pray. Amen."

Polite applause broke through the gym. I nudged the guy sitting next to me and said, "If that guy won third place last year, it's going to be a long evening." I could tell by the way he looked at me that I should have kept my mouth shut.

The emcee introduced the next speaker, and he began his prayer:

"Father, we know that time is running out. We tremble as you make us aware that we are indeed in the final days. As you have revealed to us in your book of Revelations, Christ shall come riding in on a white horse and spread his judgment among us. We tremble to think how we must account for our copious sins. Have mercy on us, Father. We stand humbly before with heads bowed, knowing that we don't come close to deserving your mercy. Amen."

I nudged the same guy and said, "That one was definitely better," – but he still gave me that same strange look.

After about ten more prayers the emcee announced an intermission. I mingled among the people and introduced myself to some of them.

"Hi, I'm John Horton. I'm from out of town. I sure find this an interesting event."

More of the same looks.

"We come here for edification," someone finally said

"We've never had strangers here before," another said.

"I'm a few hours drive from here. I saw the sign in town and decided to check you guys out." I said.

"Maybe you should have driven further."

That comment really rattled me. But it was nowhere near as rattling as what was to come. The emcee urged everyone to go back to their seats and introduced Miss Mabelle Harrison, the town's local English teacher. She, body shaking, and delivered a prayer full of good parallel structure and rousing metaphors:

"Lord, we come with open hands. We come with open hearts. We thank you that you are the bridge from you heavenly domain to our searching souls. We thank you for being the elevator which lifts us from the mire that we live in up into the celestial realms. And we have overflowing gratitude for the fact that you – even though we didn't deserve it – provided a mighty empire of salvation and didn't permit us to grovel in the sin-ridden mud of despair. Thank you. Amen.

Rousing applause greeted the prayer. Maybelle got a standing ovation. She was last year's winner.

The emcee introduced the next speaker who had a Mohawk hair cut and was dressed extremely informally. His prayer reflected his attire and haircut:

"Jesus, you're just alright. You are the grooviest savior to hit planet Earth. What a bummer it must have been for humans before you came. Thank God people are hip enough to turn on to you. How rad of you to love us like you do. Hey, Lord, that's really radical ...and groovy. You're a really "baaaaddddd" savior, Jesus. So bad that I just want to give you a big hug. Well, that's it for now, Jesus. See you around the campus. Like amen.

Polite and quick applause greeted this "Mohawk" Pray-er. The emcee introduced the next pray-er. He came up the microphone dressed in a tuxedo and black tie:

"Father, we are scum in thine eyes. We are not fit to lick your boots. Yet despite being so deeply steeped in sin, you provided – for us highly unworthy creatures – a way out of our darkness. Our souls are black with the stains of sin. Every thing we do is but ca ca, we are a swimming in pride thanking that we are good and that you are impressed. Help us out of our iniquities, o Savior! Despite the fact that we are unworthy, you have provided a way out for us. For that we will be eternally grateful. In Jesus name, amen."

In what was strange to me, this prayer got a standing ovation. Last year he won second prize.

Caught up in the spirit of the event. I found myself wanting to pray. I approached the emcee.

"I feel deep inside me the need to pray."

"We have an outsider here who would like to pray. Should we let him?"

"Let him pray," shouted most of the people; thus I slowly made my way to the microphone.

I went up, bowed my head and prayed:

"Lord, forgive me. I'm a sinner."

For what felt like it was a long time there was nothing but silence. Then, finally, someone said something:

"Is that it?"

Stirring among the people. Finally:

"Let's tar and feather him!"

"Nah, let's beat the living crap out of him."

The group slowly began to surround me. Somehow I managed to break through the mass of people and make it outside to my car. That's when I prayed another prayer:

"Please, Lord, let my car start up. I don't need a dead battery now."

I put the key in the ignition and it turned over and over without kicking in. The Horace Valley folk started pounding on my car.

"Come out, you scum. Come out and fight like a man!"

"That's the way that Jesus taught his disciples to pray!" I screamed through the window of my hastily locked car.

Some picked up a large rock and began smashing the windshield. I knew that it would only be a matter of minutes before he broke through. I then prayed my third prayer of the evening.

"Lord, help me get out of here!"

Suddenly, I noticed lightening striking all around. I looked at the man's face who had the rock. I never saw such fear. The others began backing off from the car. One of the pray-ers, Ed Gillespie, prayed again reverently:

"Lord, we come before thee with terrified hearts. Yet this man is a reprobate. Help us humble him. Cease thy angry storm."

This time more lightening struck – coming even closer to the Horace Valley folk. Timultuous thunder ripped across the valley. I turned the key, and the car finally started. I put the car into gear and inched it forward. Yet people would not get out of the way. Then I heard even louder thunder and saw that they lightening was coming ever closer.

Some of the men ran for their cars, and I used this opportunity to drive away. The cars came after me, I I could see their headlights as they moved toward me. They lit up the area around me. Somehow, I managed to get my car on the road. With terror I noticed the cars moving toward me. Then right behind me I noticed that the lightening struck a tree, having it fall across the path of the chasing cars. I kept driving until I made it to the main road.

I drove as fast I could through the windy mountain roads. Each time I saw headlights in the rear view mirror I felt that was surely someone from Horace Valley bent on coming after me.

I drove for more than four hours, making it safely to my home. When my wife and two boys returned, she asked me, "What did you do for the weekend?"

"I prayed."

2

Jesus Encounters the Growth Freaks

Jesus, on one of his infrequent strolls on earth since his resurrection, found himself in an environment that He hadn't encountered before – modern suburbia. Choosing the state of California where a rip-snorting movement had sprouted up in his name, He decided to explore one of the suburbs of the Los Angeles' San Fernando Valley. So caught up was He in the Taco Bells, Pup and Dogs, Jack in the Boxes, Der Weinerschnitzels, etc., that just for a moment He forgot his purpose to mission and walked off the main thoroughfare into the ticky-tacky of suburbia. The noise of the main streets faded somewhat, and He found himself walking down a relatively shaded cul-de-sac where the houses were more than six feet apart, meaning this was definitely a rich neighborhood.

As Jesus approached the end of the street, He was getting discouraged because no one seemed to be outside milling about for Him to talk to. Just as He was about to try somewhere else, He saw a sign which attracted His attention.

> IF YOU REALLY WANT TO GROW
> SPEND FOUR HOURS WITH US
> ON SATURDAY ATERNOON.
> NARCISSUS STREET ENCOUNTER GROUP

Aside from His hassles with the Pharisees and Sauducees, Jesus had never personally come close to experiencing an encounter group. He figured that if these people really wanted to grow, He could help them and serve mankind in the same manner He had been doing ever since His time back in Jerusalem. Consequently, He walked up to the house containing the sign and knocked on the door.

"Hi, Swami. I'll bet you're new to the neighborhood," a pudgy man said, beckoning Jesus in. "You're just in time. Can I get you a drink?"

"I don't think you understand…"

13

"Understand…We all understand. No one comes here unless he wants to grow as a human being. Right? Right. What'll it be: Scotch? Bourbon? Beer?"

"Nothing right now," Jesus said.

"Listen, everyone is accepted at face value here. If you want to play the tee-totaling act, feel free. Damned if I'm going to twist your arm. Thing is, we find that a couple of snorts really brings out the honesty. But if you say no booze – well, that's your free choice and nobody'll judge you." He then walked over to the bar, mixed a few drinks, and urged the group to sit on the floor in a circle.

"O.K., folks, just in case any of you don't know me, I'm Bill Travers and I want to welcome you to the Narcissus encounter group. Now we're sitting in a circle because we want you to feel free to look each other in the eye and say what you really feel. The point of this group is honesty, and you will be honest or we'll verbally kick your ass. First thing we do is loosen up by walking around and staring each other in the eye. We really want everyone to do this. It will loosen you up and make you free. O.K., everyone, walk around. Really look each other in the eye and, if you want to show your love to anyone, it's okay to share a hug."

The group divided itself into two smaller groups: those who were scared out of their minds because most had never tried anything like this before, and those "vets" who had been to a number of encounter groups and immediately went around hugging each other and telling them how much they really loved and accepted the other.

"I really love ya and accept ya," one said, as he embraced Jesus, digging his crew cut hair into Jesus' shoulder.

Jesus knew that the guy hated His guts because He (Jesus) was dressed in a long robe and had long hair that came below His shoulders. Jesus thought of bringing this up to him, but decided for the moment to let it pass.

"You're awesome, awesome, awesome," Janie, a housewife, cackled. Jesus knew she really meant it. However, He could also feel the bad vibes of jealousy coming from her husband who, while mixing himself a drink at the bar, was taking in the whole scene.

Jesus loved everyone there but He really didn't feel moved to get into the hugging bit, and while He felt at peace about it, a few of the people were uptight – especially those who were scared at first but decided that they better hug a few here and there so that they could consider themselves "with it." Many came up and stared right at Jesus, and Jesus just stared right back. In this action, He could gather from both the pros and the newly initiated that He was passing the test. Finally, Bill ended the exercise and they sat in a circle once again.

"Now, we're really going to get to know each other. We're going to go around the circle and I want each person to state honestly where he is with himself here and now...."

"Chauvinism, absolute M.C.P. [Male Chauvinist Pig] chauvinism," Betty White, a housewife in her late thirties, yelled out. "Come on, Bill, why do you always use the pronoun 'he'? We women are people, too."

"Excellent point, Betty. Right here and now I am a victim of my conditioning. If I should stray, bring me back gently, love."

"I love ya, Bill. I mean I really love you. But damn it, we women are people, too."

"Yes, Betty, you are…Now, I want each person to state where he or she is in the here and the now. Let it all go. If your linen is dirty, by God let's get it clean in the free spirit of this group. Wanna start, Fred?"

"My life is changing," Fred, the crew cut one, stated. "I find myself getting more and more open to change each day."

"Bullshit!" said Betty's husband, Frank. "You're nothing but some sunshine liberal who shouts about civil rights and ending the war as long as it isn't your ass. Let some jigaboo move next door and you'd be out burning crosses on his lawn. You're so full of crap, Fred. Why don't you just say what you really feel?"

"I think Fred should at least be allowed to finish," Jesus said.

"You ever been to one of these encounter sessions, fella?" Frank asked.

"Not really, but I've..."

"It shows...Now if you don't have anything constructive to add, shut up and let us get on with the business of growth."

Jesus kept quiet and listened as others threw in their two cents worth, in essence, tearing Fred apart with intermittent injections of how much they really loved him despite the fact that they thought he was not really being honest. Finally Fred admitted that he might in actuality be full of hate. This seemed to generate some instant acceptance all around.

"Hey, Fred...beautiful," Betty said, suddenly calming down.

"I see growth," Janie, the awe-struck wife, sighed.

"I feel better already," Fred stated. However, Jesus had a little problem with what Fred was saying in contrast to what he was really feeling. Once again Jesus wanted to bring this up, but felt that this wasn't the time.

"O.K.," Bill stated. "We'll move to our Swami type with the robe. What's your name, Fella, and where are you in the here and the now?"

"I'm Jesus of Nazareth and I'm..."

"Oh, that's awesome, awesome, awesome," Janie chanted.

"It's not awesome, damn it, " Fred stated. "We have only four hours and we can't screw around with horse's ass stunts like this."

"I'm really Jesus, and right here and now I have a burden for you people who are running around in circles trying so hard to find where you are."

"O.K. You wanna be Jesus, we'll play your game. But this burden-for-us crap has gotta go," Fred continued. "I mean, man, we want to know where you're hurting. Just let it all go. We all have hang-ups. How about your father...bet he really screwed you up."

"No, as a matter of fact, He sent me here to provide salvation for mankind."

No one said anything – they just looked at Jesus, as awesome-struck as Janie. Finally Bill broke a long silence.

"If you're really comfortable in this game, Jesus, okay. But I hope you find the courage as we go along to dump this mental manipulation. Anyhow, I'll play your game. Okay now. Your father sent you here to provide salvation. That's a hell of a lot for a father to dump on his son. You gotta have a little resentment?"

"No, I really love my father. We get along great. One time I felt like he had forsaken me, but we straightened that out quickly."

"I've heard that story many times before," Bill said. "What I really hear you saying is that you hate your father but you really can't admit it to yourself. I'm picking up some antipathy."

"My antipathy is to Satan. He's the one who's messing us all up."

"Satan, Schmatan. It's really your father you're pissed at," Betty said.

"O.K. You're bugged by Satan," Bill said, demonstrating his patronizing insight. "Now what I want you to do is take this club and pretend that pillow over there is Satan…or whoever is really bugging you. Now whomp the living shit out of it. And don't be afraid to scream. Scream something like 'listen, Satan, you miserable son of a bitch, I hate your guts… take that you bastard, mind-sapping miserable God damn psyche-draining son of a bitch.'"

By the time Bill was finished demonstrating the Gestalt for Jesus, he was lying exhausted in a pool of sweat. Many of the others sent out vibes of acceptance or muttered "beautiful" and "awesome."

"See how it's done, Jesus? No sweat."

"I really don't think I'd accomplish anything doing that," Jesus said.

"Well, what would you like to do? I mean who are you really, Jesus?" Betty asked.

Jesus looked out the picture window overlooking the backyard and noticed a grape arbor. "I am the true vine."

"Aw, crap, we ask a sincere question and what we get in return is a bunch of mind-fucking metaphors. Man, will you please stay in the here and the now?"

"I am the eternal metaphor and no one crashes with me," Jesus said.

"Jesus, you don't seem to get the gist of what we're trying to do here. We want to grow; and in order to grow, we can't just screw around like you're doing. Now I'm going try again, and I really want you to be honest with us. No bullshit – just honest feelings." Bill paused for just a moment and then with a strained effort at appearing gentle, asked, "What are you feeling right now?"

"Pain."

"Praise the Lord…an honest answer," Frank said.

"Pain for what?" Bill continued, ignoring the outburst.

"Pain for the coming misery that people are going to experience in this world."

"Now, Jesus, I know you're trying. But you just blew it. You see, you just jumped out of the here and now. Now let's try it another way: What do you really want to do now?…right now, Jesus…not tomorrow…not next year…not when the world is going to end…BUT RIGHT NOW!!!"

"I want to save the world."

"You want to save the what?"

"He wants to save the world!" Fred snorted and shook his head. "Let's cut the crapping around with this guy and get on to someone else."

"I think it's awesome to want to save the world," Janie said.

"You think anything in pants is awesome," her husband muttered.

Bill tried to keep things calm and stuck with Jesus despite the hostility. "Now, how is that saving the world thing working out for you, Jesus?"

"Hey, Jesus," Frank said, "what you need is a drink to loosen you up—sorta take the edge off…make you feel more comfortable. Listen–Janie makes a Margarita to die for. Got any tequila in the house, Bill?"

"I really don't want anything to drink, thank you, Frank," Jesus said.

"Listen, man, we're all hitting the stuff here. I ain't gonna have some outsider sitting there sober while I'm getting crock-ooed."

"Let it ride, Frank," Bill said. "I just want to ask Jesus a couple more questions…. Now, Jesus, what would you really like to see happen here in this room right now?"

"I would really like to see you people become free."

"Become free!" Betty yelped. "What do you think we're doing? Why do you think we're going through all this pain? Why do you think we're ripping our insides out? Why do you think we're subjecting ourselves to this mental agony? Hell, I go home really depressed after one of these sessions, but I do it because I'm learning to be free."

"But you don't need to pain yourself so much to find your freedom," Jesus said gently.

"Ah, you Bible banger types are all the same. Pie in the sky when you die. I'll tell ya something, J.C. I got a real loving inner peace and no stupid pious son of a bitch is gonna tell me different. I'm free, dammit, free…free… FREE!!! And no horseshit abundant life philosophy is going to interfere with that freedom. Got that?"

"If you're so free and peaceful, Betty," Jesus asked, "how come you have had such a bad case of bleeding hemorrhoids?"

"I don't have any hemorrhoids, smart ass."

"You're right; I just cured them."

Betty indignantly got up and walked to the bathroom so that she could empirically inspect the claim. The others just sat and stared in disbelief at Jesus.

"Now you really upset her," Frank said.

"Ya really went beyond the limits this time, Jesus," Fred said, shaking his crew-cut head back and forth.

"Christ Almighty, they're gone!" Betty screamed from the bathroom. "I don't believe it – they don't even itch any more."

She came out of the bathroom with a smile on her face and a look of peace that was strange, especially to her taciturn husband.

"What didja do to my wife? Hell, I don't even recognize her."

"I've had those things for thirteen years" Betty said "... and...zapp... they're gone. I don't believe it. How'd You do it, Jesus – hypnotism?"

"I don't give a damn how He did it," Bill said, getting mad for the first time, when he saw that the essence of the meeting was going out of control. "Now can someone bring us back to reality?"

Everyone got serious for the moment except for Betty, who couldn't resist squirming around on the floor testing the validity of her newly-effected cure. Finally, Sam, one of the quiet ones, a college graduate bachelor who had majored in chemical engineering with a minor in psychology, raised his hand, eager to volunteer what he considered to be pertinent information.

"Hey, I got it figured out. Man, it hit me like a flash as I was meditating on the whole scene."

"Share it with us, Sam."

"Yeah, Sam, really glad to hear you want to share."

"It's freaking awesome."

Everyone was downright titillated by the fact that Sam was finally going to become an emerging factor after eight weeks… that is, all except for Betty who was still wrapped up in her evolvingly orgasmic squirming.

"Tell us, Sam. Lay it on us."

"I figured out Jesus' problem," Sam said, with ever increasing confidence.

"Problem? Ha! He's got more than one problem," Fred said.

"But this is the main one. Boy, if He can get rid of this one, He can really be happy."

"Go tell it right to Jesus. Go look him right in the eye and share it with him. Tell him what you feel," Bill said, as every one began to get excited.

Sam crawled haltingly over to Jesus, sat down facing Him directly, and looked Him in the eye just like he had seen others do it. "First of all, Jesus, I want to tell you that I'm not afraid of you," Sam said with a quivering voice, "and, man, I'm gonna tell you what I think your problem is."

"Don't say 'what I think your problem is,' Sam. Say it like you really believe it."

This time Sam looked Jesus right in the eye. "O.K. Jesus, I'm going to tell you what your problem really is."

"Aw, come on already, tell him and get on with it," Betty said, apparently over her euphoria.

"O.K., Jesus, here it is. Now you probably aren't going to like this but what I say, I say out of love… You seem to be suffering from a deep-rooted Messiah complex."

Everyone leaned forward. Sam had really blossomed this time. People started murmuring at each other and wanted to explore this possibility. Everyone seemed excited except Jesus, who just sat and waited for the group's enthusiasm to wane.

"Yes, that's it," Bill said enthusiastically. "Jesus is hung up on being a Messiah."

"You can't do that, Jesus," Janie said. "People in this society when people catch to the fact that you're on that trip, they'll crucify you."

"Yeah, Jesus, start thinking realistically, and you're really gonna be happy. Hell, don't try to be too much. Be an auto mechanic, teach English. This is California; you can live on unemployment if you want to."

Jesus tried to get a word in, but it was futile.

"Man, I think we've really got to the thing that's really bothering you. Let's really probe it, Jesus…we're really on to something, now. You really shouldn't try to save others until you're ready to save yourself. I read in some philosophy book somewhere: 'Don't try to cast the mote out of your brother's eye until you're ready to solve your own problems. Great line! Who said that? Doesn't matter. What does matter is that you really hear what I'm saying," Bill said.

"Just let it all ooze out," Sam said, really paternal now. "Maybe a good rip-roaring primal scream would help. Really belt it out, Jesus–right from the gut."

"I really feel at peace with myself now," Jesus explained. "I just don't feel the need for all those things that you mentioned."

"A good schtooph, that's what you need" Sam said. "You messiah types climb on celibacy like it's some sort of panacea. Admit you're horny, Jesus. God knows, I'm not afraid to admit I'm horny. Boy, I look at ol' Janie over there and I just want to throw her to the floor and go hump, hump, hump. But we live in a guilt-ridden society and if you go hump, hump, hump you get mind-fucked by the Puritan types who lay guilt on you to the point where ya can't have any fun any more."

"You don't have to accept the guilt, Sam," Jesus said.

"Isn't that what Christianity is all about–guilt?"

"There's no place for guilt in Christianity."

"Bullshit!"

"I mean it. I don't want you to feel ridden with guilt. Your sins are forgiven."

"Don't tell me what to do with my guilt. If I want to wallow in my guilt, I'm gonna wallow in it, and no messiah type's going stop me. Besides I don't have anything to feel guilty about."

"You really feel bad about that teenage girl you slept with last Friday night. Instead of wallowing in guilt, you should be helping that girl: she's going to need someone to convince her of her own personal worth..."

"Listen, smart ass," Bill said, "I don't know who you are, but I want you out of this encounter group right now."

"Yeah, Jesus, that's really pushing it. Accusing Sam of getting it on with some teeny bopper."

"Sam, this can be the first step toward real peace of mind," Jesus said, gently.

"Just get you and your uptight moral values outta here" Sam said, more subdued now.

"You're just not awesome anymore," Janie said.

"I think it would be best for the growth of this group if you left, Jesus," Bill said. "I mean, we try to be open-minded but..."

"But you overstepped your bounds, buddy," Frank interjected.

"O.K. I'll leave," Jesus said, "but can I have just two minutes to do something?"

"O.K., two minutes, and then you leave," Bill said.

Jesus walked around to each person. He touched Frank and healed his peptic ulcer, walked up to Janie and caused a fairly noticeable scar from an auto accident to fade into the skin line, walked past Betty to Fred and healed his asthma, and then walked to Bill and touched his abdomen.

"Your liver's pretty messed up with alcohol. But it's good now," Jesus said gently and then, after encountering the rest of the people, walked into the kitchen to the Arrowhead Puritan Spring Water dispenser and changed the contents into a rare vintage of Johannes Berger Reisling. Figuring He could do little else, He walked out of the Narcissus group, up the street and back to the main road where He continued his wandering.

3

Talking Christian Head Trip Blues

They let me out of Crystal Gate – seemed like it was getting late.
Was wrapped up right in a big white coat – where dreams fly fast and fantasies float.
But I played their game and won the bout – and convinced them they should let me out.
And on the streets I'm free and clear – walking confident with no fear.
I met a guy who had the answer – jumpin' around like a raptured dancer.
"Follow Jesus and you'll know – that Heaven's the only place you'll go."
He raved on further of the joy – that came from being God's little boy.
I said, "Sure I know my life can be better – but just let me get my head together."
Farther down a guy grabbed my shoulder – and started speaking even bolder,
"If you ain't involved you're a traitor – gotta follow Jesus the Liberator.
Stop the war and all the killin' – that way your soul will soon be fillin'."
I said, "I know that society is dead – but right now I just wanna clear my head."
Then came another dude colossal – told me he was a Pentecostal.
Shouted firmly with all his lungs – "Life ain't worth it less you speak in tongues."
Said a new life could be found – then started rolling on the ground.
I said, "You can rock and you can roll – but I just want to find my soul."
Two blocks later while I was dreaming – another grabbed me and started screaming:
"God is dead and that's for sure – yet he kept saying it more and more–
He screamed so loud he seemed to fear – that God himself just wouldn't hear.
I said, "You got conviction when you strive – but me, I'm just glad that I'm alive."
Then came up this Jesus freak – and with gusto these words did speak:
"Armageddon's gonna groove – and your unsaved butt had better move,
Maranatha is where it's at – and with Jesus you can be a cool cat."
I said, "Heavy man, just let it rip – but brother, I can't buy your trip."
But finally I freaked and they took me back – put me in that jacket sack.

While squirming in that crazy game – into my cell ol' Jesus came.
He said, "I love you as you are – the game is not to make the par,
Accept me as I accept you – then to me and you, you will be true."
Then he was off in a wink – but I told this story to my shrink.
He said, "Oh golly gee," and began to shout – "You talk like that, you won't get out."
They say I'm hopeless with my clatter – but I like myself and that's what matters.
I'll remain insane I often brag – for sanity is just a drag.

4

Christianity on Five Dollars a Day

It is tragic to see Christians fret so needlessly over the high cost of Christianity. Many feel that the cost is too high. However, I say that it can be done on the cheap. Some have even gone as far as to say that Christianity should be a faith which is high in cost. However, as far as the exhortations made by some of our modern theologians, Christianity can be one of the lowest cost religions in the world – if one works on it.

We have progressed greatly since those days when even to declare oneself a Christian was inviting sure imprisonment and possible death. This condition still exists in some of the more backward countries However, here in good ol' America, one can be a Christian and pay practically nothing. In fact, if the economic structure of Christianity continues at its present rate, we might even see the day where it costs nothing at all to be a Christian.

A Good Value

Just as the American dollar has more buying power in most other countries, so can American Christianity give more for less effort. In other countries, one cannot experience the good old American joys that Christianity presents. Where else could one obtain the services of a head minister, assistant minister, choir director, and Christian education director for a mere five dollars a week? (Sure, some clock-stoppers continue to imply that one should give one tenth of his income to the Church, charity, or whatever, but still things seem to be perking just chipper at contributions significantly below that figure. While it's a shame that some ministers live on the near poverty level, their willingness to continue without complaint has kept American Christianity one of the best values per dollar anywhere in the world.)

For this five-dollar fee, the subscriber gets his choice of at least one show every Sunday morning and usually another show that same evening. Some churches throw in a Wednesday night show for the same investment. These shows provide dramatic readings by other big honchos who have the same level of training or are in the process of obtaining it. To insure variety, music is always part of the show – usually contributed by musicians who give of their time without remuneration, thus insuring that the show is able to go on at minimum cost.

While the show is considered the main effort, much more can be realized from the weekly five-dollar contribution. Included in that five-dollar effort has got to be one of the cheapest baby-sitting services in the world. For those who would rather make love during show time, the institution of Sunday school will occupy junior's mind and time for at least an hour, thus assuring that that magic moment between foreplay and coitus is joyfully uninterrupted. Many feel that this is worth the price of the five dollars alone.

But there is so much more; for that contribution also includes paid servants to "go…therefore into the world." This not only provides a cheap way to participate in the great commission, but also uniquely provides the church with a travelogue series at no extra cost. Usually a small contribution of less than a dollar toward a missionary's support insures his services to your church, thus keeping the cost of Christianity to a sane level. For this bargain fee, one can find out what is going on in other parts of the world, hear exhilarating reports on how the sword of Christianity is cutting through the jungles of heathenism, and be inspired to hear how many former head hunters and tribal chiefs have been converted to the American way of Christianity.

This fee also includes visitation insurance. Should you get sick or have to go to the hospital, one of the paid staff can be counted on to show up to spend some time with you. Times like this cause the budget-conscious Christian to want to show his gratitude and up his weekly ante.

Forget it!

If this happens, leaders will get cocky and start demanding much more, in the same manner that European hotels raise their prices when they find out that American travelers can and are willing to pay more for a room. Keep the ante down no matter how loving or guilt ridden you feel; for just as these rich Americans in Europe have ruined it for the bargain seeker, your perverted altruism will ruin it for those who are looking for low-cost Christianity.

Low Cost Does Not Just Refer to Money

Christianity has made many strides forward in emerging into a faith that requires little of your effort. In fact, with a ridiculously small investment of your time, you can still remain a Christian. You can not only experience the assurance of knowing that you'll go to Heaven after you die, but also experience all the fringe benefits of being in a Christian establishment on earth.

Christianity would cost almost nothing if it weren't for the fact that many Christian leaders still insist that Christianity is a high cost religion. These "bleeding hearts" not only insist on giving generously from their financial resources, but also invest on feeding the hungry, visiting the sick, clothing the naked, seeing those who are in prison, un-thirsting the thirsty, and taking in strangers. Where they get ideas like this, I will never know.

Whatever their hang-ups are, they keep Christianity from being the bargain basement faith that it could be. Many are getting quite militant about giving more money and especially giving more time to others in love. Yet we must hold the fort and make Christianity the low in-put, high-gain faith that it was meant to be.

Salvation Is a Gift

Jesus plainly indicated that he died on the cross to save sinners. Being saved simply means accepting a free trip to Heaven without getting hung up about doing anything in return. That's what makes Jesus such a bargain as the savior. He gave everything so that we might bask in comfort and enjoy eternal bliss. Thank you, Jesus.

Yet some still miss the message. While Jesus and Paul both indicated that man's good works were definitely not the passport to Heaven, some still insist that we ought to be out there caring about those who are hungry or helping those who are denied freedom because they are not of the white race or the Christian religion. They just miss the point. You didn't hear about the Germans executing 6,000,000 Jews, did you? No, most German Christians played it cool, kept their mouths shut, and at least outwardly endorsed Hitler's National Socialist policies. Because of this, they endured little or no pain during the Second World War. Consequently, they not only had the assurance of eternal life should they have been killed by a bomb or stray bullet, but life for the most part was pretty uncomplicated – as long as they kept their mouths shut. Had only men like Diethrich Bonhoeffer followed this method instead of living up to his insistence that the cost of discipleship was high, he might be alive today.

Now you see why you are lucky to be a Christian in America. Christians need not feel they have to pay a moral debt just because our society is really hurting in many areas. Christians need not suffer the abuse that minority groups attempt to inflict on them. Christians need not feel guilty that others in the world are poverty-ridden or haven't had a meal since God knows when. Christianity, if practiced with the right mental set, can be the least demanding faith one will ever encounter.

Consider our society. True, someone should be doing something about the social ills that plague America; however, the Christian who knows his Bible and theology well can free himself and his fellow Christians from any obligation simply by utilizing a few mental realities:

(1) Jesus is probably coming soon. (Read The Late Great Planet Earth) Thus, any effort would probably be futile.

(2) God loves being praised, and praising God is much easier than loving someone who probably hates you in the first place. (Note George Bush and most right wing conservatives.)

(3) Getting rid of hunger and improving prison conditions definitely isn't fulfilling the Great Commission. (Matthew 28:19)

(4) Most people you help don't really appreciate what you do for them anyway, and Jesus told us not to cast our pearls to the swine or give what is holy to the dogs. (Matthew 7:6)

(5) Being with people who are in a despair-ridden situation does not contribute to personal joy. (Philippians 4:4)

(6) Getting involved in social issues might make the church appear more relevant than it really should be and thus attract more undesirable people into the fold.

(7) Loving our neighbor is what we're paying our spiritual leaders and missionaries to do for us.

Finally, Christians, you need not feel guilty because other people in the world are starving or experiencing strife. Our priority should be to pray that God will help them. Put it out of your mind and thank God that you have enough food. Now I don't want you to think that I'm saying that we should avoid the hungry completely. A contribution to the Overseas Hunger Relief Fund really isn't a bad idea every once in a while, and baskets of food for poor families during Christmas or Thanksgiving is a tremendous witness to God's love.

Jesus pointed it out so well when he said that man cannot live by bread alone. Still, some say that Christians by nature are greedy and unwilling to share their food. One need only witness a low cost church supper to see what a ridiculous accusation that is. For those concerned that nothing is being done to help the starving and homeless, consider that part of your five dollars sometimes goes to the missions and food centers in all of our cities. You can't do any more, so relax.

Concerning strife…well, that's where Christians have the upper hand. Even if one lives in a war torn land, he still has the assurance of a restful life after death. Christians in America have had hardly any strife at all, and as for concern about wars in other lands, instead of fretting over the fact that man's sinful nature manifests itself in other places, just thank God that you are not part of the problem.

For those Christians who feel that killing is altogether wrong and that we as Christians should make a stand on this exhortation from the Bible, let me remind you, God many times urged mortals to go and kill other people. Be honored that God has called America and a few of her lesser friends to wipe out Iraqis, al' Queda, and all other Satanic forces. When some Islamic rabble-rouser blasts off, claiming that we are killing innocent women and children in the Middle East, just say, "Get thee behind me, Satan" and walk off in the assurance that your Christianity is solid and showing forth what it really is.

In order to insure a low cost Christianity, you are going to have to avoid these problems completely. Christianity is not stress, tension, or concern: these factors very frankly get in the way of the fun that Christianity was meant to be. One cannot enjoy Bingo sessions, skating parties, the Women's club, the church choir, and the main show itself if the body of Christians keeps on insisting that it get involved in other peoples' problems.

Now, I want to be practical and suggest ways that you can keep your Christianity down to what one would metaphorically refer to as a "five dollar a day level." For those who are feeling in a particularly magnanimous or altruistic mood, I have a section called THE BIG SPLURGE. For those who find that the "five dollar a day" level is too costly from the standpoint of involvement or concern, you will find your needs fulfilled by the STARVATION BUDGET section. Also in this edition, to show you the tremendous possibilities that are within Christianity, I will conclude with CHRISTIANITY ON NOTHING A DAY. Considering that Jesus paid a lot by dying on the cross, we do hope that most of you Christians will be good sports about the whole thing and stick as close as you can to the "five dollar a day" program.

Also, Christians need not suffer any consternation because many minority groups claim that Christianity is racist, non-involved, and insensitive to the needs of oppressed minorities. Fortunately, most inner city churches have had an amazing degree of precognition in sensing when these minority groups might make things hot, and quickly remove themselves from the problem. From both a moral and monetary standpoint, all benefit. The minority group gets the physical church plant for much less than it's worth, and the original moving people go out to an area where they are sure of obtaining more people who are willing to come through with their five dollar a week ante – all benefit. From both a moral and mental standpoint, those who would have left the church anyway can now retain both their friendships and their peace of mind. Out in the suburbs, they won't have to hear about black Jesus's who embrace the black power fist, but instead continue to admire their blue-eyed, blond-haired Jesus in his spotless white robe.

For those who feel some guilt about the fact that Christians don't do enough for those minority people and fear that their cries against American Christianity might be just a bit valid, reinforce yourselves with the following realities:

(1) We have missionaries in Africa.

(2) Part of the five dollars helps black people, Indians, etc.

(3) Black Power is not Christ-centered.

(4) Blacks have their own Christianity.

(5) If God had wanted us to be compassionate to Indians, he wouldn't have let us slaughter them in the first place.

(6) Indians still continue to worship heathen gods.

(7) Chicanos and Puerto Ricans can turn to the Catholic Church. No, the priority of Christians is to do as little as possible and get as much as possible from their investment.

We have no intention of leaving you without some solid practical advice. People who are genuinely concerned about the fact that they may be paying too much for their Christianity have written and asked if there is any practical plan available. Thus, to be absolutely sure that you do the least possible and not one jot and tittle more, I do. It is similar to the travel book that insures that you can have a wonderful vacation in Europe by not spending more than a certain amount of money for your room and the three meals each day. My plan assures you as a Christian that you can spend as little as possible and still make your Christian commitment seem like a vacation. The plan works from this basic skeleton:

A. Attending church about once a week

B. A weekly contribution of five dollars

C. Token efforts at loving your neighbor.

A lot of people might get angry at the inclusion of church attendance in the plan; however, one must consider the practical values. First, this lets your neighbors know that you are a Christian. Should they have had any doubt before because of some of your other actions, this should certainly clear up things. Also, it lets those who are members of your church realize that things are just A-okay between you and God. You certainly wouldn't be going to worship God if things weren't A-okay, now, would you?

Should your relationship with God be just a little strained, He'll certainly notice that you're doing your part by coming to church, and next time when you ask for something you really need, He just might be more inclined to see it your way.

In the church service, you also take care of two of the items mentioned in the Big Splurge portion of this chapter: prayer and Bible reading. During the service, this is taken care of already; thus, you need not make an expenditure of concern over the fact that you didn't pray or read your Bible during the week.

Other practical factors should be considered. Your presence lifts the morale of the minister and his staff; and with a high morale, the staff thinks less about raises or rising above their poverty level. It also gives you the mental satisfaction of doing something in return for the fact that Jesus died on the cross for our sins. And don't forget that you meet people whom you might not only make as friends but also who could be very useful to you in relation to your business or financial affairs. I know some people whose weekly contact has tripled their five-dollar a week investment from friends saving them money or from gaining business contacts.

The five dollars a week has already been covered and is the financial aspect of Christianity's cost; however, Jesus did talk about loving our neighbor as a cost of Christianity also. At this point, a lot of people express concern because they think this means unscriptural things like loving your enemies, loving the unloved, reaching out to our underprivileged brothers, etc. Concern thyself not, Brothers; loving your neighbor can be accomplished with little effort.

Begin by picking out people who are safe to love. These people can usually be found right within the confines of your own church. You just can't love everybody, so you may as well stick to the ones who make it easy. As far as the unlovable and underprivileged are concerned, love them every once in a while if it will make you feel any better. However for God's sake, don't get involved. That will only wear you down and make you less lovable to those who already love you.

Now if you're still hung up about those poor unloved and underprivileged people, just remember that there are a lot of bleeding-heart liberals around who are doing more than their share of screwing up the Christian economy, even though many of them are not even Christians in the first place. Don't let those pinko do-gooders cause you to stray from your path. Do your part and no more.

True, some of the minority groups are going to moan that Christianity is too lily-white and really doesn't have much compassion or relevance for colored people, Chicanos, Spics, etc. This of course is a bunch of crap: Jesus had all types in his little disciple group. However, if the antagonist won't listen, bring him over to your church to see the contributions that just your small body of people is making to city missions, missionaries, etc. If the antagonist still persists, tell him you won't buy any lettuce the next time you go to the supermarket or that you are going to urge your church to make a contribution to one of the black Christian colleges. That should do it.

Don't under any circumstances do any more – for this will only cause more to be expected. True, circumstances happen where a man might not have eaten in three days and perhaps it wouldn't hurt to make a rare exception by giving him bus fare to get to the mission. However, this expenditure should be deducted from the five-dollar ante. Other times, you might see someone cold, shivering, and lonely and be tempted to walk up and offer companionship. Don't! Just call the mission in town, and someone will come pick him up. After all that's what the church's money is paying for.

Starvation Budget

Some of you are probably saying that what I have mentioned under the five dollar a day plan is just too much to expect of a Christian and that you are definitely going to pull out if these demands continue to be made. Fret not! God loves you just as you are, and you can still be one of his children with minimal output while reaping all the benefits.

Under the starvation budget plan, you make it to church about once a month so that the people see you and know you're still interested. When you do attend, put a dollar or two in the plate. While this doesn't come close to the five-dollar ante, you still have the satisfaction of contributing to the Lord's work without the financial drain. In addition, you have the benefit of all the aforementioned benefits without the financial burden.

Concerning participation in the token efforts of loving your neighbor, perhaps putting some spare canned goods (nothing more than beans or corn, mind you) in one of the charity boxes, which you find in your local grocery store every once in a while. That shouldn't hurt. If you are one of those guilt-ridden types who insist on making an expenditure of personal effort instead of money, then smile at your neighbors as you drive off to work. If you're really gung ho, help some old lady across the street. However, don't go beyond that, or we'll have that nasty old social gospel back in power again.

The Big Splurge

This section is for those who every once in a while really want to be super Christians. If applied with temperance and infrequency, it really isn't that bad a thing. Some people will insist that this section represents where Christianity really should be, but even the early Christians had their zealots We have survived in spite of them.

The big-splurging Christian first of all intensifies his witness by going to the Wednesday night service. Yet other people should never be encouraged to think that this is going to become a habit. If there is no Wednesday evening service, then try the Sunday evening service – if you can take two church services in one day. If a Sunday evening service exists and the hymns are really fun to sing and the anthems really top notch in musical quality, go to both morning services, leaving before the sermon in the second service if it is really that bad. If your church does not have two services, you really aren't getting all those terrific advantages for your five-dollar investment and should find another church.

The big splurge offers the opportunity to be magnanimous at certain moments; though these should never be overdone. Assume you've already made your five-dollar investment; yet you hear a touching story of African kids who come eagerly to hear about the Lord in a roofless school. This is movingly related by a missionary who has to teach out in the rain half the time. If you're moved, throw a dollar into the special plate – but only if it makes you feel good. Or perhaps the minister is inspired to take a collection for flood-ravaged victims. Throwing in your spare change will enable him to expound that Christians really do care and can be counted on when the going gets rough.

If you're really feeling super, try reading the Bible along with a little prayer. Although some radicals say that this should be done every day, you should remember that you are paying the minister to take care of these things.

As far as loving your neighbor, here's where your effort can shut up those rabble-rousing liberal Christians. Be bold – take a black or Chicano out to lunch. Be a chaperone on the next youth fellowship retreat. Take a basket of food to the poor when it isn't Christmas or Thanksgiving. Cut a good two feet farther when mowing the lawn so that your neighbor will know that you can really be generous, and offer to look after the neighbor's dog as long as it won't be longer than three days. However, whatever you do, make sure that these actions don't even come close to becoming habits. Sure, you're going to feel good about such magnanimous gestures, but not only will you eventually cool down but also your spirited altruism may screw it up for the rest of us. We don't want people to gain unrealistic expectations of Christians – definitely avoid going overboard no matter how good the feeling.

You shouldn't have more than three or four big splurges a year. That's enough to show that you can do more than those liberals who bitch and moan with no effort and it's enough to show you that as a Christian – you can love your neighbor even if you don't feel like it.

Christianity on Nothing a Day

Christianity need cost nothing at all if that's the way you'd really like to have it. You need not go to church at all; in fact, more and more putative Christians are catching on to this idea. (Some go just Christmas or Easter for guilt insurance, to keep their foot in the till, or both.) You still know you're going to Heaven and you can always show up for a performance when it looks particularly good.

Most churches will let you be members even if you don't contribute a red cent. True, there will be harassment for about six months; but if you hold firm, eventually the financial forces of the church won't bother wasting the money for postage in letters to you.

And you can love your neighbor without being involved. In fact, withdrawing from the situation completely not only minimizes the cost of involvement, but spares you the possibility of being lured into feelings of hate for your neighbor. This process is called "love at a distance." Just keep your distance from the young, the oppressed, and the militantly vocal minorities as well as other forces that you deem undesirable. Ask nothing and expect nothing in return – except maybe to tell whoever might be threatening you to keep his place – which really isn't asking that much when you get right down to it.

If you start to feel guilty about this no-cost Christianity and feel that you should be doing something more to manifest your love, get your thoughts under control and realize that you can't carry the problems of the world on your shoulders. Face the reality that whatever is happening to your neighbor is probably God's will anyway, and you definitely don't want to meddle with providence – now, do you? No, just by keeping your nose out of things, you'll be compensating for the overt actions of those do-gooder liberals who insist on being hung up on the idea that in witness and involvement Christianity is a high cost religion.

You can be a living testimony to the contrary.

Praise the Lord.

5

Television Relic 666

Script from Videotape December 31, 2009

Tom Brokaw: Ladies and gentlemen, we are situated here on a remote island off the coast of Sri Lanka to witness what could be the most significant moment in the history of Christianity or, for that matter, world history – the fulfilling of the Great Commission of Jesus Christ. Thirty-eight years ago, in June of 1972, nearly a hundred thousand people gathered in Dallas, Texas, to train and prepare for the fulfillment of the Great Commission. Most ignored the vision of a physically small man, Bill Bright, President and founder of Campus Crusade for Christ International. Even in this year of '09, people scoff and mock; but as far as we know on the last day of this year, all peoples of the world will have heard the Four Spiritual Laws – with the exception of a hermit who has lived alone for thirty years off the coast of Sri Lanka.

A penetration team is now making its way to share the Four Spiritual Laws with this recluse, and thus fulfill the great Commission by the end of this year. This event is so momentous that all networks have joined together to present it live. Now for a report on the intense saturation campaign of Campus Crusade for Christ and the Four Spiritual Laws, I turn you over to my colleague network, Richard Engle. Come in, Richard.

Richard Engle: Thank you, Tom. And you crystallized it well, for this is truly an event of great magnitude. Five years ago this reporter was a skeptic obsessed with self-glorification. What did I know; I was too young and spoke Arabic and I was really full of myself. While on the outside gleamed the shield of self-confident arrogance, inside was a welt-schmerz, which cried for fulfillment. I will not forget that day when Peyton Manning pulled out this little yellow book and said, "God loves you and has a wonderful plan for your life." Of course, I thought he was being facetious and I immediately said, "Cut the crap, Peyton," but I could tell by his expression that this was not a typical Peyton Manning altercation. For once he was serious and explained how man was separated from God yet how he provided a way for man to encounter God. That day, this reporter got down on his knees and prayed that concise little prayer–and things have been hunky-dory ever since. Rachel

Maddow and Brian Williams both remarked about the change the first time we got together to report on the situation in the Middle East. But now to the business at hand. This year we have seen a momentous event take place. In the past, during election years, our nation's youth have campaigned for their favorite candidates. This year, young people have been traveling all over the world to share the Four Spiritual Laws with those who have not heard. The aim: to fulfill the Great Commission; in other words, tell every living person in the world about the saving power of Jesus Christ. Now all have heard. The promulgation has been inspired, the reaction varied–as pointed out in a special report.

Tom Brokaw: All have heard…all, that is, but one. But what has been the reaction? This film report gives you an idea of some of the response. Roll the clip, please….

Woman One: Oh, Praise God! My life has been changed. Eight years ago, little Freddie Martelous came back from Explo 72 nearly 30 years ago. I couldn't believe the change in the little son of a (bleep). Always swearing and getting his nose in things. This time he came over with the Four Spiritual Laws and read them to me. I could see that there was a change in this little…. this boy. His face actually glowed, and I was so moved that I prayed that little prayer in the book, and things haven't been the same since that wonderful time..

Man One: I can't believe that people would believe all that (bleep). We've been oppressed by those white crew-cut mother (bleep) for over three hundred years and now they want to push their (bleep) (bleep) Jesus right down our (bleeping) throats.

Man Two: Gotta admire their guts, goin' out and stating what they believe. Damn refreshing, that's what it is – the good old American spirit of selling your product no matter what. Just like good ol' free enterprise.

Man Three: Praise Jesus! I was about to shoot up some coke when this good-looking chick said that God loved me and had a plan for my life. I told her that I had a plan for her body, but she told me I needed the body of Christ. She was right and I came over. Now we're married and I have both bodies.

Woman Two: It's all right if you like that kind of stuff. Each person should do his thing, I guess.

Tom Brokaw: According to Bill Bright, people's opinions are not that important. The important thing is that the world hears. That was the command that Jesus gave and now with the exception of one lonely hermit on a tiny island off the coast of Sri Lanka, all have heard. Brian Williams is on that tiny island with a report.

Brian Williams: I'm standing here on the Island of Obbu off the coast of Sri Lanka at the coordination center that is attempting to find Aratus, the hermit who left the mainland of Sri Lanka thirty years ago to live in the wilderness. Three days ago, the Campus Crusade for Christ organization was about to acclaim a fait accompli as far as the Great Commission was concerned; but the Sri Lanka International Director remembered that Aratus was out in the wilderness. Since he left before Campus Crusade came to Sri Lanka, the chances are fairly good that he has not heard the Campus Crusade for Christ's Four Spiritual Laws, or some reasonable facsimile that would affect the needs of the Great Commission. At this point, search crews are combing the jungles trying to find what appears to be a most reluctant Aratus. The imperative to get the word to Aratus today before 2009 passes into 2010 is strong: a lot of cynics would like to see Campus Crusade for Christ miss attaining the Great Commission by 2010. However, one thing now does appear to be quite certain: famous psychic Sonia Moores' prediction that the Great Commission would be accomplished on February 18, 2010, at 5:23 Eastern Standard Time appears to be a bit too far projected.

Tom Brokaw: I don't mean to interrupt, Brian, but our old friend Anderson Cooper is standing at the other end of the island with some significant news.

Anderson Cooper: Thank you, Tom. This could be it. Search party 312 has found and apprehended Aratus Obandu, the only living person who has not heard about Jesus Christ and the Four Spiritual Laws' plan for potential salvation. The apprehension of this man was not without cost: one of the members of the team was bitten by a cobra and, in his dying delirium, true to the goals of Campus Crusade for Christ, read the Four Spiritual Laws to an elephant. Whether the elephant was moved to a spiritual commitment, we have no way of knowing; but we do know that the man who died stuck to it to the end.

Brian Williams is now with the person who will read the Four Spiritual Laws to Aratus Obandu.

Brian Williams: Tom, I'm here with Maybelle Fridge of the Wycliffe Bible Translators. She learned sixty-three of the sixty-six dialects of this surrounding area and that makes her best qualified to wrap up the Great Commission. What do you say, Maybelle?

Maybelle: Well, ever since I broke my engagement and decided to go it full time for the Lord, I knew that He had something special for me.

Brian Williams: And you're going to talk to him as soon as the tranquilizing drug has had its effect. In fact, I've gotten word that he's calming down a bit.

Maybelle: Right, Brian. I'm going to read to him a translation of the Four Spiritual Laws as soon as I find out what dialect he understands.

Brian Williams: I've heard that he's ready now. Ladies and gentlemen: this could be one of the greatest moments in history, certainly the greatest moment in the history of the Christian Church. Maybelle Fridge is walking up to Aratus Obandu with a copy of the Four Spiritual Laws. In just a matter of minutes the Great Commission will be history. I'm going to walk over and catch this great moment.

Maybelle: Obbunti chanti oglindana fuchu machandizi.

Aratus: Machandiziz fiszu omp ompinfi bow wow.

Brian Williams: I presume that Maybelle has said, "God loves you and has a wonderful plan for your life" in Aratus' dialect; however, her face is getting red and she seems quite taken aback by the reply of Aratus. Maybelle, can you give us the gist of what Aratus said in reply?

Maybelle: I….I….I really don't think I….I….I'd better.

Brian Williams: Well, could you give us a refined or loose translation?

Maybelle: Well, it went something like "Get lost, you fornicating female Fox Terrier."

Brian Williams: I guess you would surmise that you are not being too well received.

Maybelle: I've had many who started out hostile but at the end, they prayed that little prayer, some of them bawling like babies. The battle isn't finished. I have three more laws to read to him, so it isn't over yet, Brother Brian.

Brian Williams: Maybelle is returning to where Aratus is being restrained and reading law number two stating how man is basically rotten and definitely needs some help from above. Aratus is screaming rather vehemently and from the tone of his voice and the contortions of his face, I would gather that he isn't saying, "Praise the Lord."

Aratus: Unfangu, unfanga, ichiziza unfangu.

Brian Williams: Maybelle, we seem to he hearing this word "unfangu" a lot in your conversation. Could you give us an idea of what this word means?

Maybelle: John, this is one of those words that is hard to translate literally; however, it relates distinctly to the fecal matter that emanates from the male cow.

Brian Williams: In other words, "bullshit?"

Maybelle: I would prefer to think that in the literal translating it has more the impact of "bull feces."

Brian Williams: Maybelle is having a hard time reading the fourth and final law because he keeps shouting the same phrase over and over again. Maybelle, can you give us an idea of what "Frigandizi guasi" means?

Maybelle: Oh, John, it's so horrible. I had hoped it would go so much better than this. This is a fine how-do-you-do for wrapping up the Great Commission. He ought to have his rectum thumped and the poo poo knocked right out of him.

Brian Williams: Well, what's he saying?

Maybelle: It's not worth repeating. Besides, I've found it physically impossible to do it to myself anyhow. Oh, my goodness!

Brian Williams: Aratus has broken away and is running into the depths of the jungle. People are running after him, but I've never seen a man run so fast. They'll never catch him the way he's going. Right now, Campus Crusade officials are conferring, trying to find out whether Maybelle actually got through the fourth and final law. It's a tense moment because the way Aratus was going, they won't find him for another ten or twelve hours, and that would be too late to have the Great Commission fulfilled by 2010.

Now, I've received word that one high ranking official of Campus Crusade for Christ has wired to Bill Bright asking permission to bomb the area where Aratus is hiding, on the theory that if Aratus were dead, then all living people would have been reached for Christ in 2010. I hear among some of the lower echelon and even some of the higher echelon of Campus Crusade staff prayers that, if it be God's will, a cobra or lion might attack Aratus and help Campus Crusade for Christ save face as this year 2010 trickles away. Word comes to me that Bill Bright has replied to officials' plan for bombing the area in much the same manner that Aratus replied to Maybelle's reading of the fourth spiritual law.

Wait a minute, a momentous decision has been made. By a vote of thirteen to two, the staff members here have decided that Aratus heard enough of the Four Spiritual Laws to get the idea of what was going on. Thus, ladies and gentlemen, just moments ago you witnessed the fulfillment of the Great Commission. I now return you to Tom Brokaw in New York.

Tom Brokaw: Here in Times Square, people are filing into the street singing "Praise the Lord" and "When the Roll is Called Up Yonder." Not all is harmony, however. Some apparently still feel that the Great Commission has yet to be fulfilled, and other militant voices have taken up the chant of "unfangu," indicating, along with the fleeing Aratus, their views of the whole situation. If the Great Commission has indeed been fulfilled, then we must speculate when Jesus will return. Jimmy the Greek has laid down odds that it will be sometime in the year 2020. Hal Lindsay, author of "The Late Great Planet Earth," says 2017. Anyhow, alternate cries of "Come soon, Jesus" and "Unfangu" now emanate from Times Square. Should Jesus come rather soon after the fulfilling of the Great Commission, we will be there covering it first hand. Whether T.V. cameras will be permitted to cover the rapture in the skies can only be left up to conjecture: however, if Billy Graham and Bill Bright are right in what they say, many of us will be left behind, and we urge those of you to stay with the network of your choice right up to and through Armageddon.

For those of you who can't tune in locally for one reason or another, that's the way it is. This is Tom Brokaw, good night.

6

A Somewhat Modest Proposal

At 180 degrees, it struck me. Behold, a new ministry. I had been running around the indoor track of the Beverly Y.M.C.A. trying to get myself to the point where I could run two miles straight, and I had barely made a mile; thus, I made my usual retreat to the sauna hoping that it would rejuvenate me.

Now if you haven't been in a sauna, what I'm going to explain might seem a little vague. A sauna is a tremendous relaxer and rejuvenator; however, to get to this point of relaxation and rejuvenation, one goes through a period of discomfort as his body adjusts to temperatures that range from 170 to 220 degrees. The body sweats profusely and there is usually shortness of breath in the first stages. The first few times can be particularly uncomfortable when one breathes that hot air into his unaccustomed lungs. While one conditions oneself to these discomforts, he never really gets used to them. It was while going through this period of discomfort that God revealed His plan for what I hope will be a Christian institution: THE SAUNA MINISTRY.

Consider the fantastic potential of such a ministry. First of all, believers will arm themselves with the Word of God and then join Spas, Y.M.C.A.'s, athletic clubs, etc. The only prerequisite is that they have a sauna. I figure the training and preparation to be about three weeks in good grounding of belief, sharing methods, testimony presentation, and the like. That would be Stage Alpha.

Stage Beta would consist of getting to know people in these organizations: in essence, building up their confidence in you as a person. The art of winning and losing gracefully cannot be stressed too much, as well as good sportsmanship under all conditions.

Now here comes the important part: Stage Omega. Actually Stage Alpha and Beta are basically worthless if they don't lead up to Stage Omega. Stage Omega IS the sauna ministry. It is simply a conversational method that should bear much fruit.

What one does is go into the sauna just after someone else has preceded you by five minutes. That person should just be hitting the point of discomfort. Then you walk in and sit there saying nothing for about two minutes. That allows enough time for your body to be a little bit uncomfortable while the other guy is really suffering.. Then you open up.

"Hot as hell, isn't it?"

Our subject, in most cases, will nod in agreement. But you can't let him control the situation. You now come through with Stage Omega, Part B.

"Have you ever thought about how hot hell really is?"

Most men will answer with, "If it's this hot, I sure don't need it" or "I don't know, but I hope it ain't this bad."

At this point, I would recommend an appreciative chuckle. That creates empathy and shows that you're an alright guy. Let the subject express his misery, for here the timing is essential. He will be hitting the ten minute mark: the point of highest discomfort. It is essential that you have had enough experience in the sauna to know when that point is coming. When you do see it coming in the subject, hit him with plan C of Stage Omega.

"You know, I'm never going to know how hot hell is." Now this particular wording is essential because the subject's concentration will be waning with the increasing discomfort; thus, the alliteration of "how hot hell is" is needed to make its punch.

This punch established, the responses should range from a vociferous "Who the hell are you to say that you'll never find out how hot hell is" to a meek "You sure are lucky. How can I be sure that I won't have to face an agony like this?"

No matter how the person responds, Stage Omega, Part B, is the ideal time for you to slowly rise and say to the subject:

"I am going to the cooling waters of the shower. That's just fifty feet away. We both have that at our disposal. But I already have the cooling waters of eternal life -- you don't. If you will accept these cooling waters, your greatest agony will be right here in this sauna; however, if you reject the cooling waters of life eternal, then what you're sitting through now will seem like a cold shower when you face the flames eternal."

Don't wait for an answer. Retreat to the shower and begin singing "Safe am I" in a lusty, happy voice. If this doesn't bring him out, try a chorus or two of "This World is Not my Home, I'm Just a-Passin' through." Chances are very strong that he will come out and ask how he can have that eternal water. Sometimes you might have to wait until he turns on the relieving waters of the cold shower. Watch his relief and then soothingly state:

"If you think those finite waters are soothing, wait till you feel those eternal waters."

In most cases, that should just about do it and another one should be brought to the fold. However, we should be prepared to face the fact that a few will not accept what we have to offer and not get bent out of shape about it: we can't win them all.

But I do see great things for the sauna ministry. I see those reached being trained and reaching others. Amateur athletes will come in contact with semi-professional athletes, and semi-professional athletes will come in contact with professional athletes: all because a few brave men are going to boldly speak forth in saunas all over the country. Once the big athletes have been reached, they will see the error of their ways in pushing shaving cream, beer and other sorts of worldly things. Then, like these charter few who began the sauna ministry, they shall speak forth on T.V. and many shall be made aware.

Can't you see it now? American Idol is half way through its show and into its fourth commercial break. On the screen, at seven feet two inches, stands Shaquille O'Neal practicing dunk shots. Then he slowly walks over to the drinking fountain, stops, and looks at the camera as it slowly focuses on his face.

"You know, I used to think that a cool drink of water after a hard work-out was the best thing around. But one day after a tough game I was sitting in the sauna with Pat Robertson...."

7

The Big Game*

For the past eight years, the two rivals had been battling each other. Whoever came up with the idea that the Liberal and Conservative Christians have a yearly football game to determine supremacy in the Christian world is not really known; however, despite their intense rivalry, neither team had won a game in the past eight years. In fact, neither of the teams had scored a touchdown.

Nine years ago the conservatives won the game in the final quarter by falling on a fumble in the end zone. The score was 6-0, conservatives. Ten years ago the liberals won 6-0 when they intercepted a pass and ran untouched the five yards into the end zone. Both teams were convinced that they lost the game because they were weak and decided to go apart from their original game plan.

Today, both teams felt something in the air, and despite the fact that every game including this one was a sell-out and they had prime-time T.V. coverage, an electricity pervaded the air revealing that today something might happen to break the scoreless deadlock.

The Conservative team reflected its theology in the way it played football: their attack centered around running; however, good blockers were hard to find since a top quarterback named J. C. Gottenmann, the team's original quarterback of years past, did it all alone, scoring touchdown after touchdown, while the rest of the team hovered fearfully and safely in the locker room. This year's top quarterback, Big Billy Cracker, admitted time after time that he was nowhere near as good as J. C. Gottenmann and constantly pleaded with the Conservative team to work on their blocking. Still, the Conservatives considered themselves a running team despite the fact that Big Billy screamed at them constantly for their refusal to block.

* Thanks to Tony Presser (who wrote the Introduciion), for his input into this story. –J.B.

Oddly enough, the Liberal team had just as many problems. First of all, they claimed that J. C. Gottenmann played for them; but they could never agree among themselves whether J. C. scored touchdowns as an example to them or simply because the rule book said that was the thing to do. In fact, they spent a lot of time arguing about that when they should have been playing football. One of their favorite stories concerned the fact that J. C. Gottenmann really didn't score any touchdowns at all, but instead got mauled badly while running for the goal because he stopped to help a puppy that was limping across the field.

Many gathered from this action that scoring touchdowns wasn't really relevant and thus figured they should spend the bulk of their time looking for dogs that had been crippled. In fact, they spent a lot of time making up cute posters with cute slogans about how loving it would be to help limping dogs – the best being a poster with a picture of J. C. Gottenmann in his football uniform holding a panting dog with a bandage on its right hind leg. However, despite this effort, many crippled dogs still walked the streets.

The forte of the Liberal team was defense. Yes, they had held the opposition scoreless; but they had one heck of hard time finding players who wanted to run the ball. It didn't seem to bother them at all that they had not scored. The team also was the only team to have a female member, thus advocating women's liberation. This was Maggie O'Flair, who had the paltry task of placekicking, and Maggie sure was a kicker. She not only kicked the ball over the goal post with every kickoff, but also kicked along with Gloria Hammenstein, the water girl, about the fact that there weren't more women playing on the team. However, the Liberal team informed them that they had really moved ahead by having Maggie as a player, that the Conservative team didn't have any women on their team, and to shut up and kick.

Maggie once again boomed it over the goal posts and the Conservative team had to start on the twenty-yard line. Big Billy Cracker marshaled his forces.

"O.K., men, we can win this one if we really play hard and especially if you all block. I'm going to hand the ball off to Skinny Tom on the left side."

"Let's have a prayer," the right guard said.

"Let's block hard and then we can pray," Skinny Tom, the team's only black player, said.

"Blasphemy!" another lineman yelled.

"Ya gonna play ball or pray all day?" Tommy Oldhauser, the Liberal team's halfback, screamed from the sidelines.

Finally, as the team came out of the huddle, a rousing cheer boomed from the Conservative side of the stadium. The center hiked the ball and Billy handed off to Skinny Tom, who was mauled five yards behind the line of scrimmage.

"You guys gotta block!" Big Billy screamed when back in the huddle.

"Should of prayed," the right guard muttered.

"J. C. Gottenmann didn't need no blocking," the left tackle said.

"Now look," Billy said, "I'm going to run around the left end. Do you think you could give me some blocking?"

"I'm praying for ya, Billy."

"Do you think you could block along with your praying?"

"I don't know, we ain't never run around the left end before. Better stick to the old plays."

Nevertheless, Big Billy ran around the left end, despite the fact that Skinny Tom was the only one to block for him. Billy actually gained a yard and a half. However, he had gotten mauled pretty badly and fell down twice while limping back to the huddle, where he found the rest of the team singing joyously about the fact that he had actually gained yardage.

On the next play, Billy could have gained about a yard, except for the fact that he tripped over two of his players who were cowering in fear, and instead had to kick to the Liberal team. As the ball soared high in the air from the kick, the members of the Liberal team immediately began communicating among themselves.

"You get it!"

"No, you get it!"

"Not me."
"Somebody's gotta get it."

"Guy could get hurt."

Finally, Bart Tilly fell on the ball. When he got back in the huddle, he began berating the rest of his team members. "You guys are chicken! We're not going to win this game unless someone has the guts to run the ball."

"You're beginning to sound like one of those Conservatives," the left end said.

"You wanna win the game, don't you?"

"It's not whether you win or lose, it's how you play the game."

"Oh, that's terrific, Hamilton – did you think that up all by yourself?"

"Don't get smart with me, Tilly. We've mauled their team, and we should be proud of ourselves."

"A couple of touchdowns might help us win the game."

"There you go again with that touchdown crap. If you're so damned hung up on touchdowns, why don't you go play for the other team?"

"Does anyone want to run the ball?" Tilly asked.

"Why don't you run it, smart ass?"

"I'm a lineman."

Because the Liberal team couldn't find anyone to run the ball, Ruddy Neatbeer walked up to the line of scrimmage and began screaming about how the stories of J. C. Gottenmann were really myths and that he didn't really play for any of the teams. Some of the Conservative members pulled out their history books (which they always carried with them) and began reading accounts to Ruddy. However, Ruddy wasn't impressed and continued his tirade while the referee inflicted eight straight delay-of-game penalties and put the Conservative team in good field position. The Conservatives took over without a play being run by the Liberals.

"Come on, guys," Billy Cracker pleaded. "We're closer to the goal than we've ever been before. If we can move twelve yards, we'll score a touchdown."

The right tackle stared in awe. "Look at them goalposts. I never seen them this close before."

"Let us pray," the right guard said. "If the Lord wants us to cross that goal, I'm sure he'll show us the way."

"Faith without works is dead," Skinny Tom reminded them.

"Who said that?....Is that some of your black revolutionary dogma which you're trying to bring into our camp?"

"James said it."

"James who? James Meredith?"

"James in the Bible."

"You're putting me on. Bible wouldn't say a thing like that. How come I never heard it before?"

Billy put his hands to his head and squeezed. "Think we can play ball?"

"You sure that's what the Lord wants?"

Billy thought about turning the other cheek, decided he was already sore enough on both of them, and sent Jack the Wart, the other half-back, around the right end. At least, the Wart started toward the right end, but was mauled a split second after Big Billy handed him the ball.

"There's a blessing in everything," Jack the Wart said. "When you get mauled behind the line, you don't have far to walk back to the huddle."

"Praise the Lord!"

With barely restrained piety, the right guard said, "I don't think the Lord wants us to score a touchdown."

Bonner Dietrich, the fullback, nearly exploded with apoplexy. "Horse manure!"

"You watch that foul language, Brother Bonner. If you can't be a witness and a good one, you can go play for the other team."

"Just might do that."

While all this was going on, the fans on both sides were wild with ecstasy: chanting, yelling and singing. Suddenly, Billy started talking over the public address system.

"We need your help, you people in the stands. We can't do this alone. The rules are flexible enough so that anyone in the stands who wants to play can suit up and join us on the field. I urge you now to come down here and work with us."

"That guy's really pushing it," one of the Conservative fans muttered. "We come here to have some fun and he asks us to work. I paid five dollars for my ticket. What more does he want?"

"Ol' Billy ain't the same what he use to be. He's a sellin' out to the dang Liberals. Rumor has it that he's a sayin' that the Conservative team should get down there and block."

"Really?"

"Really."

"What's happening to Christian sport? It just ain't fun no more."

Big Billy Cracker walked dejectedly back to the huddle and made another plea. "Guys, if we're willing to get hurt a little now, we can win the game. We're only fifteen yards away. We can do it!"

"J. C. Gottenmann is coming back soon, ya know. Why don't we call time out and see if he comes back in time?"

"Yeah! I got proof right here that says he's definitely gonna come back and play for us again."

The right guard ran up to the referee and called time out; then all the linemen sat together sharing different proofs that J. C. Gottenmann was really going to come soon.

"Guys, J. C. Gottenmann isn't going to come again until we do our job."

However, the group continued sharing proofs and then singing about how great it was to be on the Conservative team, totally incognizant of Billy's and Skinny Tom's shouting, as well as the fact that they were pushed back beyond the fifty yard line with all the delay of game penalties.

Eventually, the Liberal team took over and Bart Tilly tried to rally his forces. "Men, if we run now, we'll floor 'em. They won't know what hit them."

The left guard snorted. "I'm having more fun mauling the sons of bitches!"

"Gotta be relevant. It ain't relevant to run. We're changing – can't you feel where the people are going?"

"Yeah, if you want to bitch, Bart, bitch about the Conservatives. They can't even get anybody to block. They're really screwed up, you know."

"Yeah! Bunch of chicken turds! If they think they're so great, why don't they block like we do?"

Bart Tilly shook his head. "The idea is to win the game."

"That sounds awfully Conservative to me."

"You wanna win the game, don't you?"

"Cool it, Bart! We aren't going to win people over to our side if we tell them they gotta run."

Ironically, while the Liberals bickered, the enthusiasm continued to mount in the stands. Neither faction had any doubt that their side was winning the game, despite the fact that no one had scored in a very long time. Then, a limping dog painfully made its way across the field.

"Somebody ought to help that dog," one of the Liberal players said.

A Conservative player scratched his head. "Think that dog knows about J. C. Gottenmann?"

"Look at those Conservatives! Not even making an effort to help the dog!"

As a matter of fact, no one made an effort to help the dog, as it finished its agonized limping and walked out of the stadium. However, it was a mangy dog and could be smelled twenty yards away.

The Conservatives started a chant they never seemed to get tired of:

> "We've seen the light
>   Our cause is right
>   We'll fight the fight
>   With God's great might!"

Some of the Liberals claimed that J. C. Gottenmann originally left football because he couldn't stand the repetitive monotony of the cheers. There wasn't any documented evidence to support that idea, of course, so the Liberals developed their own cheer:

> "Dogs, dogs, dogs…
>   Their bones have no fat.
>   Feed the little puppies…
>   That's where it's at."

Both sides felt that the other side's cheer was absolutely disgusting. Some of the more objective observers in the stands thought both of the cheers were disgusting and began wondering whether the rumor about the cheers driving J. C. out of the game had any credence to them.

Although no one in the stands responded to Billy's or Bart's calls for help, the fans from both sides began to pass around literature urging people to join one of the teams. They considered that to be "playing the game" and thanked God for the opportunity to demonstrate that their faith was real. Those who remembered to pray also remembered to thank God for those who were down on the field getting the living crap kicked out of them.

The main problem was that both sides spent more time yelling at each other than they did actually playing football. The fans hung in there anyway.

The center for the Liberal team shook his fist, figuratively casting the first stone. "You Conservatives spend too much time running the ball. And when that poor little doggie limped across the field, all that one of you did was go up and hand it a set of first aid instructions."

Figuring that a second "stone" was better than no stone at all, one of the Conservative players responded. "You Liberals waste your time mauling us because you're afraid you'll lose the favor of the people and not be relevant. I didn't see any of you helping that puppy. Besides, helping puppies is not what we're about."

And so it went.

The Conservative team used all its time outs in the first quarter because they wanted to pray. The Liberal team resorted to screaming at the Conservatives instead of running the ball. Bart Tilly, during one of his tirades, did produce some impressive statistics showing how many stray puppies had been lovingly cared for, and Ruddy Neatbeer and Tilly Barth almost had heart attacks when Billy and Skinny Tom admitted that puppy care should be part of the game.

In the stands, the fans were continuing to have their fun. Each side would scream vociferously when their team would take time out to try something new. The Conservative fans sang song after song, whereas the Liberal fans preferred chanting. Though the game was only two-thirds of the way through the first half, it was already dark in Gehenna Stadium. Seven hours had passed, but nothing had abated the enthusiasm of any of the fans. What none of them seemed to notice was the fact that no one had turned on the lights and the playing field was no longer visible.

It didn't matter. Nothing was happening there anyway.

8

A Radical Christian Looks at Explo 72

Those who forget the past are condemned to repeat it.
—George Santayana

In Dallas's Love Airport, a salesman, frustrated at his failure to rent a car, secure a taxi, or gain accommodation, summed up what a stranger might have felt about Explo 72.

"What's going on here? You can't get any service. This is worse than a convention."

"The Jesus people have taken over," the Avis girl answered.

"The Jesus people? I didn't know there were that many."

There were that many. On the second night of the six-day conference, the Cotton Bowl was not only filled to near capacity in the grandstand areas, but also tens of thousands of high school "delegates" sat down on the football field itself and all eyes in the Cotton Bowl focused on an elevated stage at the east end of the field.

People who wanted a good seat knew that they had to arrive before six o'clock, and a significant number of the seats were filled by that hour. By 7:00 when the action was to officially begin with music and "sharing" by Jesus-singing groups, any seat that offered a view of the proceedings was taken. When nothing happened up in the stage area, these "delegates" from all over the United States and at least sixty countries found plenty of vociferous activity to pass the time.

"Two bits, four bits, six bits, a dollar;
All for Jesus stand up and holler."

Most did. They just never seemed to get tired of this one. "Praise the Lord!" one side of the stands would chant, in a spirit which exceeded even the best efforts of support for the Texas or Cowboys football teams.

"Amen!" the other side would respond.

The seats at the Cotton Bowl were fine as long as you weren't over five-foot six and didn't have a waistline of more than thirty-six inches. Any dimensions beyond either and you were in trouble. Since something happened about every three minutes to merit a standing ovation, my six-foot six-inch frame was given some relief; although I did have to wedge my 40-inch waist out from between the arm rests at times.

The Jesus gospel group, Andre Crouch and the Disciples, came on the stage and worked this crowd into a frenzy, which eventually would require a plea from Billy Graham to calm down so that the T.V. audiences, for which they were recording, wouldn't get the idea that this was some ego-tripping, hell-raising venture. As Andre's melodies intensified, so did the involvement of the masses. "One way" signs flashed all over the stadium; people swayed en mass to the music. If you weren't tuned in to the spirit of the moment – waving arms and all – well, you just sorta stood out like someone who refused to stand up when the Star Spangled Banner was being played.

The band below, The Explo Honors Band, never did play the national anthem, but they did belt out one version of "Amazing Grace" that had the masses singing in such intensity that it must have been heard in the nearby city center. Everyone knew "Amazing Grace": we can thank Arlo Guthrie for that. Later, the masses sang "Oh, for a Thousand Tongues to Sing," which was introduced as "Oh, for a Hundred Thousand Tongues to Sing."

No matter where one stood on the theological spectrum, one had to be impressed with this gathering. The vision of Campus Crusade's director, Bill Bright, had come into fruition. Explo 72 was more than just a gathering of 100,000 Christians for fellowship; Bill Bright saw it as the Holy Spirit's gathering of people to begin the final steps of fulfilling the Great Commission of Christ. Just so that no one got confused as to when this was going to happen, 1976 was established as the date for the United States and 1980 for the world. What this meant in essence was that every living soul would have the chance to hear about Christ and have the opportunity to receive Him as Savior. As soon as I began hearing the numbers and the dates, I began wondering whether I had mistakenly walked into a Kirby Cleaner Convention. But I kept my hopes up.

During each day the "delegates" were trained in how to share the claims of Christ through a booklet known as "The Four Spiritual Laws." This booklet has the message of Christianity condensed into intense brevity about the same way that Lipton's soup has things down to just dehydrated powder, vegetables and noodles. Near the end of this booklet is a little prayer all made out that, supposedly upon using, provides instant Christianity. Despite my personal distaste for this "freeze dried" approach to Christianity, it seems to work in some situations – at least for the moment; however, other times it leaves people with a "cheap grace" faith that is high on euphoria and low on commitment.

From Tuesday, June 13, to Friday, June 16, the nearly 80,000 delegates were to meet (after scattered conferences all over town) at the Cotton Bowl for a mass meeting. From 7:00 to 8:00 P.M. the meeting consisted of music. From eight o'clock on, the official meetings were to begin.

Tonight's meeting began with an introduction of the sixty official countries, and the delegates from each county stood up while a flag bearer marched on the field below. Mexico had the most; however, Korea had an amazingly large delegation. If anyone wondered where Explo delegates were politically, the cheers that went up for the introduction of South Viet Nam would have allayed any doubts. They received a standing ovation without any dissent at all. That frankly scared me a little.

Following this introduction, the various directors for selected countries came forward momentarily to share their successes in the name of God and Campus Crusade for Christ. The Nigerian director told how the president of the student body was just one of many who were making decisions for Christ. The director from West Berlin told of a girl who was about to commit suicide but instead read the "Four Spiritual Laws" and "decided that she wouldn't destroy herself." The director from Honduras said not only that great things were happening, but that he wanted prayer that they would fulfill the Great Commission by the year 1978–two years ahead of the world, but still not one-upping the United States.

However, the ultimate in chutzpah was displayed by the director of the Taiwan Campus Crusade for Christ ministry who kept insisting that he represented the China delegation. Cheers greeted him as he mentioned that at every Chinese University, not counting those over on the mainland, of course, there was a group of students who were getting together for Bible study. Cheers nearly drowned out the announcement that every day Chinese students were turning from their own religions to that of Christianity. And cheers overwhelmed the Cotton Bowl and its environs when he mentioned that they were going to take the gospel to that other place that lay to the west of them. Somehow they never got the gumption to mention the name of that other country. My friend Rick remarked that this reminded him of a 1933 meeting of the Free German Youth when Hitler was starting to come into power. I shared the same feeling. It was turning into a Christian head trip with shouting replacing committed contemplation. I looked in vain to find evidence that this night's session would show that evangelical Christianity could rise above the hoopla that has been both a shield and excuse for the lack of involvement in the problems of society. It seemed like it was the same old trip with many more people.

The announcer stated the statistics for the various groups and mentioned that a little less than half of the delegates (about 35,000) were high school students. I began to be a bit concerned and felt uneasy. Who would guide these people gently down from their high when the conference was over? Who would lift them after they crashed from the joy of the moment? Who would give them the wisdom to understand that it would be terribly difficult to explain the beauty of this moment to their friends who hadn't been there? In my work with Christian groups, this has emerged as one of my greatest concerns–how do you keep people from crashing from the high of the moment?

The moment of ultimate bliss came with the introduction of Billy Graham. This just might have been the most vocal response Billy ever received. He could have been Der Fuhrer; but fortunately, he didn't choose to play that game. He did boom out ten reasons why Explo 72 might be the most important event for Christians this century. With each exhortation, the cheers became more intense until, with the last one, Billy stated that Christians would now be on the march. Then mayhem ruled. I could see those kids goose-stepping out of the Cotton Bowl behind Fuhrer Billy; however, at this moment, the leadership of Bright and Graham seemed to know better, despite the fact their wisdom was not emulated by the delegates. The people whom I worried about were the teenagers down on the football field. They were grooving on the Blood of the Lamb, but I couldn't detect any sense of real gutsy commitment – just grooving.

In all fairness to that particular group, they appeared to be impressing a lot of people. Down on the field, they were an amazingly well-behaved group with amazingly little running around, unless they were dancing to the music of one of the Jesus bands. The director of the Cotton Bowl was "amazed" at how "relatively clean" these high school students were in cleaning up after themselves after eating, and this was an effort to feed thirty-five thousand people. At the empty end of the football field, a group of high school students sat in a perfectly formed cross that was at least twenty yards long. However, I had to ask myself the question that plagues me more and more in relation to organized Christianity: are these kids being fed or are they just being momentarily titillated? I have seen too many young people get psyched up only to be psyched-out two or three weeks later. Moreover, that minority of non-Christians who were not into this particular Christian trip must have had one hell of a time.

The emcee mentioned that this gathering would go down as the greatest student gathering of the century – a little super-optimistic, but no worse than I've heard at some political conventions. Then he asked anyone who either slept on an air mattress or on the floor to stand up. At least half of the high school field bunch stood up as well as a significant number in the stands. The estimate was that about a third of the people at Explo were NOT sleeping in beds.

"Anyone who doesn't have a bed meet at gate two. If you come down, you can sort of take up your bed and walk," the emcee announced.

The emcee then mentioned that they were going to hear from a number of professional football players from the N.F.L., who one-by-one walked up and introduced themselves with cheers for each one – but great intensity for the Miami Dolphins. [Miami has won the Super Bowl the previous February.] Finally, Bill Tripplett of the Baltimore Colts gave his testimony:

"In 1962 I felt the greatest thing in my life would be to play for a professional football team; however, there was still a void in my life and it wasn't until I lay on a hospital bed in 1964 with tuberculosis that I came face to face with Jesus Christ..."

Tripllett knew the right things to say and evoked much applause; whereas Roger Stauback, who could throw passes beautifully, wasn't as adept at throwing out the "that's-what-I-want-to hear" evangelical clichés. Good heavens, it took him almost two minutes before he even used the name Jesus; though when he did, a few started to get with him. But he still insisted on speaking in a way that was comfortable to him and thus, despite being the quarterback of a world champion team, he had to take second seat in the "rouse-em-up-for-Jesus" category.

Finally Billy Graham came out once again and urged the masses to cool it on the "Praise the Lord", "One Way," "Hallelujah" type cheers and sit "absolutely still and reverent" because Bill Bright was going to speak not only to the eighty thousand in the Cotton Bowl but also to a potential audience of 35,000,000 on some delayed tape broadcasts. I guess the noise wouldn't have fit in or the editing would have been difficult. However, the message turned out to be so mundane that the words of Billy Graham became superfluous.

I guess Bill Bright figured that he had a choice: stimulate and challenge the 80,000 in the Cotton Bowl or appeal to the mentality of those who would by-pass network T.V. to watch this broadcast. His choice was almost instantly obvious and thoroughly tragic for the people in the Cotton Bowl. Having been scheduled to speak on the Great Commission, which I consider one of Bill Bright's best talks (that I had heard two times before), I urged my friend to come down with me. So instead of a third run of the Great Commission talk, I received the perennial rerun of how-to-be-saved-from-sin jazz, which had as its only proximity to uniqueness the fact that "maybe you've accepted Jesus a lot of times before but this should be the last time."

In my boredom, I looked down at the white band that circled my left wrist. I looked upon it as my Albatross, as I was sweating in this area. At registration I was told not to take it off because if I did I wouldn't be able to put it back on again – shades of Auschwitz and Buchenwald – you're going to be a witness for Christ whether you like it or not. If you don't have your band on, you won't get your discounts from the restaurant. During these moments I couldn't get my mind off this. Even in the Explo official program they tried to make humor of the situation by showing a cartoon of a guy who had lost circulation in his hand; however, despite the humor, the written admonition was just as strong: "Once this bracelet is placed on your wrist, it must not be removed for the rest of the week (after it is taken off it cannot be refastened)." No matter what the intent, I got the message: you take off that wristband and it's your ass.

Bill Bright finished his talk and gave the opportunity to pray to receive Christ, and then asked those who had asked Jesus into their lives to stand up. Not many stood up from the grandstand section; but it appeared that half of the field section of high school students stood up. Immediately, questions began to plague me:

"Were there that many who were 'non-Christians' (or at least non-evangelical in their approach) in that group?"

"Were these just part of that Jesus people trip of getting saved over and over again every time an opportunity presents itself?"

"Were these the same people who were singing, shouting, chanting, and flipping alternate claps and one-way signs all through the evening – if so, were they then just caught up in the spirit of the moment?"

"If it were the spirit of the moment, were these people just following it or genuinely making a conscious rational decision for Christ, or perhaps both?"

"Was this the work of the holy Spirit or mass hysteria?"

I don't have any problems in believing in the Holy Spirit. If this were an emotional sham or at least had tinges of it, the Spirit might work with it or perhaps in spite of it. With that little assurance, I put it out of my mind and went home.

Wednesday June 14th

I had started the day with the intention of attending some high school and faculty conferences, but a state of confusion between what was the Hilton Inn and the Statler Hilton plus the notoriety of Dallas traffic control quickly frustrated this goal. Thus, I rode around the city and its suburbs just to experience the impact of Expo 72. I knew that evangelical exaggeration would assure me of the tremendous impact at the Cotton Bowl sessions, but I wanted to see it for myself.

Driving around the city and eventually out into the suburbs, I realized that even with the expected evangelical exaggeration I would hear, the impact was at least visibly impressive. On every corner in the city, groups of people walked with the badge of EXPLO 72 and the ever-ubiquitous white wristband. (I did see a couple people along with me who had taken the damned thing off, and [true to the warning] they could not be fastened again.) Even though it was not an official "share the gospel" day, many were out in force sharing from the booklet "The Four Spiritual Laws."

Out in the suburban north area on Hillcrest Road, I saw three young girls stop a maid on her way to the bus and immediately begin sharing "The Four Spiritual Laws." The poor woman looked just a little bit trapped and somewhat embarrassed by the whole thing, but I'm sure the girls had no doubt at all that this was where the Great Commission was centered. Up a few more blocks, I stopped and talked to a group of six high school students who were planning to spend the whole summer saturating the Dallas area with the gospel. I couldn't help but admire their guts and zeal – their sincerity couldn't be doubted. What did concern me was their "If they don't think like us, they're full of shit" trip. They spent a lot of time condemning Parkins Theological Institute and its professors because of their more liberal views, but they never really got nasty. In fact, it was a genuine concern that, while it reeked of "those poor sons a bitches" mentality, it was still genuine.

What they did have was a sense of commitment that I rarely see anymore…especially when one lives in Southern California, the national capital of non-commitment. They had a purpose which few people under eighteen rarely touch. When someone responded to Christ, they were happy for that person. One old lady, who at the outset had refused to talk to the kids and eventually yielded, came back repeatedly to thank the kids "for witnessing to her." If this deep commitment to a shallow evangelistic endeavor could move into a commitment to pay the price involved in Christian Agape (Love), we will see and notice the change; but these beautiful, idealistic and committed kids need responsible leadership to inspire them beyond the superficial "evangelizing" rut we have fallen into.

* * *

Tonight's meeting was contrastingly subdued in relation to last night's Jesus pep rally. For one thing, an early morning driving rain had thoroughly soaked many of the high school and college kids. In addition to this, many understandably stayed up late in their newfound freedom and by evening found that "jumping and shouting" didn't come as easy as before. The emcee also urged that the cheers be kept down once the eight o'clock "Son Session" began.

Billy Graham came out once again to say just a few words to the troops:

"I want you to know that the owner of the Cotton Bowl told me that last night's crowd was in his opinion the best behaved crowd in the history of the Cotton Bowl. He also said that when a function is over they usually have truckloads of trash; however, last night, they found only two pieces of trash.... What I want to know is who those two people were who left the trash."

Bill Bright's wife, Violetta, spoke briefly on the reality that our country is in a period of decline and that only a spiritual revolution could save it. What followed was definitely a spiritual decline for Explo 72.

Since June 14th was Flag Day, Campus Crusade decided that they should at least acknowledge the event. Problem was that they did more than acknowledge the flag – they bought the age-old assumption that the flag and the military are somehow coordinate and thus ornamented the ceremony with high ranking military officers, astronaut Jim Irwin, and some prisoners of war wives. A general from the U.S. Army opened by mentioning that today was the 197th anniversary of the United States Army and embellished this statement with the explanation of how it came about as an Act of Congress. Many critics of the Jesus movement believe that it is ripe for a right wing take over: the action down on the field seemed to give some support to this. Whether right wing or not, it was certainly in bad taste.

High in the grandstands in the empty seats behind the stage sat members of The People's Christian Coalition – probably the most radically left, evangelically Christian group in America. Quietly they draped down two signs: "CROSS OR FLAG" and "COUNTRY OR CHRIST." Their intention was to make a quiet protest; however, the tastelessness of the moment must have angered them for they began chanting, "Stop the war, Stop the war, etc." When they stopped, they were greeted with intense hissing from the high school students down on the field. That incident, to put it mildly, scared the hell out of me. Images of the free German youth were no longer titillations of a mind that occasionally brinks on the cynical; but were real fears that this zeal could so easily be channeled into a "Nail a commie for Christ" mentality that could gain the church support that Hitler seemed to have no trouble getting in pre-war Germany.

A group of policemen rushed up to the group of about thirty people. However, it was Christians who said to the policemen:

"Leave them alone; they're our brothers."

When it comes to wisdom and love, some came through and revealed that Christ really does made a difference in spite of personal differences.

The session continued with more national directors giving accounts of what was happening with Campus Crusade and Christianity all over the world: tales of converted communist student leaders juxtaposed against Hindus who gave their lives to Christ. Meanwhile, in the area of the Peoples Christian Coalition, people were coming over to confront, speak to, or evangelize the members of the group. A Baptist minister in a coat and tie looking as straight as a minister could look stated that he was ready to go to jail with them if it came down to that. Others expressed genuinely pleasant shock that evangelical Christians would even take a stand on the war. Reporters from major T.V. networks were planning interviews with this very atypical group. The fact that this group, which combines social and spiritual commitment in Christianity, is so atypical is what really depresses me about both liberal and conservative Christianity.

After some group singing and a fantastic rendition of a modern translation of First Corinthians Thirteen, Bill Bright went into his talk on love. To say that Bill Bright improved one hundred percent over his previous evening's talk would be detrimental to Bill Bright's effort tonight. It was more than a significant improvement. Tonight, he challenged instead of titillating. He at least urged love as part of his talk and mentioned the futility of all the other hoopla if it was not based on love.

However, we weren't going to get by the evening without some good old-fashioned titillation. E.V. Hill, a black pastor from Los Angeles, started out quietly enough and at times even reeked of wisdom. However, after about five minutes of relatively quiet admonition, he began playing to the emotions of the audience. As callous as this may sound, he reminded me of what I had learned in my speech class about Adolph Hitler! Begin quietly and gradually build up to a fever pitch. He was right on that track. As his speech intensified, so did the reaction of the audience: hand clapping evolved into vociferous shouting; inert forms proceeded to wave their arms with the One Way sign.... which looked a lot like "Heil Hitler." The louder it got, the more I got turned off. I didn't feel these people at this point were praising Jesus–instead they were once again wallowing in the blood of the lamb.

As E.V. Hill ended his talk, he had his audience at such a peak that all were standing and shouting in an emotional frenzy that contained little rationality. I guess I should have been thankful that it was "Jesus...Jesus... Jesus" instead of "Deutschland Uber Allies" or "Today Germany...tomorrow the world," but I still was scared.

In the midst of the frenzy, Bill Bright came back to the podium and quietly reminded them that emotion is not where it's at, but love was where it was at; and he alluded to the earlier presentation of Corinthians Thirteen. It took the wind out of a lot of sails; it took the zeal from the moment; it took a lot of guts. However, it was essential. Bill's words ended the evening, and the masses walked out of the Cotton Bowl in a sober and reflective mood, many singing old-fashioned hymns.

Thursday June 15th

With Bruce Bonecutter, one of the leaders of the People's Christian Coalition, once again I rode through the streets of Dallas. My purpose was still to see if the evangelistic effort was indeed being effective; his was to sample the feeling of typical delegates toward last night's "disruption."

As far as the press was concerned, they appeared to opt for pleasing the masses and in one way or the other condemned the outburst by the most subtle means of chicanery.

"I don't think politics or the war has any place at this convention," one delegate was quoted as saying. "We're here to share Christ."

Two other delegates were quoted as being against the war, but both agreed that the shouting was out of line. Neither these two nor any of the other quoted people seemed to feel that the use of the military and their pro-military remarks were out of line. No, sirree! This was a conservative convention in a comparably conservative city.

We picked up a group of four delegates from Virginia. Immediately they began by asking us our opinion of the fact that some Jesus freak rock bands including Love Song and Larry Norman were having their own show and "getting in the way of the purpose of Explo 72." Since this was the first time I had heard of the intended concert, I could only state that the counter-culture-oriented Jesus people really couldn't feel too comfortable, stimulated, or even edified within the confines of the super-straight Explo structure. Because a couple of them had used the term "counter culture" like it reeked of feces or other bad things, I really wasn't surprised when they didn't understand what I was trying to get across, but they were quite disturbed about the effort, despite the fact that I found out later that it had been secretly planned by Campus Crusade for Christ, interestingly enough, as an alternative to Explo 72.

"What did you think of last night?" Bruce asked, in an effort to be as unobvious as possible.

"Great, great," one of the girls stated.

"Was there anything at all that bothered you?" Bruce tried again.

"No," another one of the girls stated.

"Got a little emotional instead of spiritual the first night," one of the guys stated, "but that improved the second night."

"How about the protesters?" I finally asked.

"Protesters?"

"Oh, I know what you're getting at," one of the girls said, looking at our black armbands and having a moment of astute revelation.

"I don't think they showed much wisdom disrupting things. Our purpose here is to share Christ…," et al.

And on it went with the exception of being told that no one could go to a rock dance concert and keep his mind on God. We let them off and two of them politely informed us that we were instruments of God because just a few seconds before we came along and offered them a ride, they had asked God for a ride. Praise the Lord! Right on!

As we cruised deeper into suburbia, we noticed a group of high school students had virtually taken over a three-block area. As we cruised by, they gave the "One Way" sign and shouted, "Praise the Lord." They gave me the impression that they were saying God's forever fraternity was a groove and as soon as you learned all the secret grips, you'd feel downright "in."

We decided that we would let some of these high school kids do their thing on us; thus, after taking off black arm bands, Explo badges, and the "irremovable" white wrist band, we pulled up to six students and asked "What's going on here?"

"Have you ever heard of this?" one of them said, pointing to the "Four Spiritual Laws" and not really answering the question.

"What's that?" I asked.

"This is God's plan for you. Let me read it to you. We call this 'The Four Spiritual Laws' and you can see here that it says 'God loves you and has a wonderful plan for your life.'"

And off we went as water was poured into the freeze-dried food pouch.

To be honest, both of us were impressed with the guts and sincerity of these kids, despite the fact that many times they stuck tenaciously to the Four Spiritual Laws (which they were instructed to do) and answered our feigned skeptical questions with canned clichés that must have been meaningful to the speaker but had little meaning for the beholder. But in this frame work they were beautiful kids, and we had no doubt that each one of them really loved us and, in their way, really wanted to help us. We really hit them hard. And while they were scared, they hung in there to such a point that I began to feel bad about the put-on grief they were getting.

"You sound like you're pretty skeptical about all this," one said, slightly understating the point.

"Why aren't your friends helping you?" I fired back. "It looks like they're letting you do all the dirty work."

"No, they're praying for me."

"Doesn't look like they're praying to me."

At that point, some of the others came over, and they stuck with us, answering all our "nasty" questions with a boldness that I enjoyed seeing and hearing. In fact, they were so beautiful and so loveable, when one of them said "It's wrong when you do something sinful like cussin," I stifled the urge to say "What the hell's wrong with cussin?" And when we told them that we felt getting it on with chicks was a wholesome and neat thing to do, they showed an amazing lack of legalism by stating simply that if we put Christ first in our lives, "Well, there's just a chance that you might feel differently about it." These kids had it together – they were ready to go into the arena. Someone should tell them where it is and how to get there.

When we finally told them that we were actually in their camp, they sighed a breath of relief that created a gentle breeze. They were full of joy and didn't seem to have any negative feelings at all that we were putting them on. In fact, we saw two of them at the Cotton Bowl that night, and they glad to see us again.

Being curious about grass root reaction to the People's Christian Coalition, I joined Bruce for a couple of hours in front of the Cotton Bowl, selling their paper, The Post American, which, while dealing with a Christian approach to social issues, did hit strongly on the war in Vietnam.

"Are you the people who disrupted the meeting last night?" so many of them would ask.

When we answered in the affirmative, they were amazingly cool about their bad feelings toward us. Some opened their Bibles to Romans Thirteen and read the following to us:

"Let every soul be subject to the higher powers. For there is no power but of God. The powers that be are ordained of God. Whosoever resisteth the power resisteth the ordinance of God and they that resist shall receive themselves damnation."

It was dreadfully out of context; whereas an exegesis of "Love your enemies" didn't make an impact at all.

"When you go against the war in Viet Nam, you go against God's will," Cal, a student from Georgia, told us. "God gives everyone power; he even gave power to Adolph Hitler."

"You mean to say that Naziism and the liquidation of six million Jews was God's will?" I asked.

"It's all part of God's plan, and we shouldn't stand in God's way. You certainly believe that God founded America, don't you?"

"No, I don't believe God founded America."

He found that a little hard to digest, but he hung in there, refreshingly free from condemnation of us as people, despite his intense antipathy to what we stood for.

Every once in a while, a radical or leaning radical Christian would walk up to us and state how glad he was that the People's Christian Coalition was at Explo 72.

"Man, you really restored my faith," a student from South Dakota stated. "I really am solid in my Christianity, but I've always felt that it leaned more to America than Jesus; yet when I share this, people really put me down. And when I state how immoral I feel the war is, they just turn me right off. It's a bad scene."

Many were downright shocked at seeing that this "leftist" oriented paper was in fact Christ-centered. Because of that, people were surprisingly receptive to looking at the paper and contributing a nickel, dime or quarter to help cover the cost of the printing. This was pretty good when one considers the fact that every type of Christian literature – the whole spectrum of the Christian circus – was being pushed on these people.

The Pentecostals were everywhere passing out leaflets stating that getting saved, committing your life to Christ, being baptized, and all the other things that go with the evangelical experience, just weren't enough. According to the pamphlets they were passing out, there was a final step to knowing that you've arrived in the Kingdom of God: Speaking in Tongues. (This, referred to as glossilalia, is a gift of the Holy Spirit in which the receiver of the gift speaks in seemingly unintelligible tongues. According to Scripture this gift is to be used strictly for the glorification of God – preferably when someone who has the Holy Spirit's gift of interpretation can interpret the tongues. Many evangelical Christians feel that urging everyone to speak in tongues goes contrary to Scripture.)

* * *

A rainstorm which began shortly after six o'clock marred the Thursday Cotton Bowl session. I'm sure many of the near hundred thousand delegates felt that good old God just wasn't going to let it rain while the "Son Session" was in progress, but it did. The emcee stated that Texas was in dire need of rain; thus, this was a good thing and probably an answer to prayer. Someone to the right of me remarked that God should have had it rain in the afternoon and left the evening skies clear. He really had it figured out.

Billy Graham came out and told the people that Bill Bright would give a brief message then they could go home. Believe it or not, the near capacity crowd groaned – especially the area of the ever-zealous gung-ho high school students who were sitting down on the field where the waterproof tarps that protected the field were retaining every drop of water. Still they were packed tight as ever, refusing to let the paltry chemical combination of H2O deter their spirit in any way. In fact, Billy Graham continuing his rush of superlatives, stated that he had never seen a crowd stick through a rain storm like this crowd. Score another one for Explo 72.

Try as hard as they did, the rock groups tonight didn't have a chance; power shorts, excessive feedback, and the rain itself thwarted any effort to get the crowd involved – except the high school students on the field who would have hung in there even if the speakers and amplifiers began blowing up and throwing sparks out into their midst.

What was tragic was the fact that tonight was pledge night and envelopes with pledge cards, maps of the intended Great Commission, etc. were intended to inspire people to give both their time and their money for this effort. What happened was that the envelope turned out to be a good seat cover and the three-by-four-feet Great Commission map made an excellent umbrella – for about the first twenty minutes Then it futilely collapsed, leaving the delegate who was not blessed with an umbrella in wet despair.

Bill Bright came out and told the people that he was going to give an invitation for those people to stand up who would promise to do anything that Christ asked them. He urged that all who remained (significantly more than two thirds of the people) to think about this seriously while he talked, so that what they did, sitting or standing when the chance came, would not be an emotional thing. Thus he explained the need for people to commit themselves to the will of Christ and asked those who would be totally open to God's will to stand.

Of course, the masses stood when the invitation was given, and I'm sure many really meant it with a total willingness to be open to God's will; however, emotion rather than commitment seemed to win the day. It was the thing to do–to stand up in rain instead of taking a stand under more difficult circumstances, to make the big emotional commitment of the moment in the Christian Circus rather than the moment by moment commitment that is needed in the Christian arena, to groove instead of move. Yes, it was moving, but would it cause movement?

*   *   *

Leaving the Cotton Bowl, I went to the People's Christian Coalition Booth. One of the girls I had talked to, who had laid Romans 13 on me, and felt that the Coalition was out of line in shouting "stop the war" last night, was back inside the booth talking and listening seriously with one of the Coalition people. On the outside of the booth, a staff member of Campus Crusade for Christ was driving home his concerned point.

"It's a greater sin to tell a half truth than it is to tell a lie and your organization is only telling half of the truth."

"What do you mean that we're only telling half the truth? We believe that we're telling people much more than they hear from other Christian organizations and we're still emphasizing the point that a person needs Christ. We're not taking away from that at all."

"But you're claiming that we are wrong when in fact it is the communist nations that are wrong. It is those countries that are going to be judged by God. You should be mentioning that."

"We don't really believe that. We believe that what we are doing is also bad."

"But we've got to stop communism."

"The way we are doing it is immoral. We are not actually stopping communism."

"Well, I want to tell you that I love you, and at least you're on the right track."

As he walked off, I took my rain-drenched body out of the exhibition hall and in the direction of my car.

"Hi, brother, praise the Lord," a student from Kansas greeted me, and began talking about how great Explo 72 was. "This is fantastic, isn't it? Christians coming from all over the world to share the love of Christ and witness."

"It has its moments," I said.

"It's fantastic the way that this city is being affected. People making decisions for the Lord. You can really see the Lord at work. Hey, how come you're wearing that black arm band?"

"It's the band of the People's Christian Coalition."

"People's Christian Coalition?" he said, as if he had meant "Commies for Jesus." "What's that?"

"It's a group of Christians who believe that Christian commitment should extend into the social issues of our day and particularly feel that Christians should not support the war in Viet Nam."

"Are you the people who yelled at the meeting last night?"

"Yes, we are."

He then looked down at his feet, trying to conceal his disgust, and then turned around and looked the other way. The conversation was over.

Outside, Bruce Bonecutter stood by the road hitchhiking in an attempt to get back to where he was staying.

"Praise the Lord," four girls shouted as their car whizzed by.

"One way," two college guys yelled, as their half empty car went past us.

"Jesus loves you," a couple more shouted as they flew past.

This went on for an hour and a half. Finally, after just about all the delegates had passed by, a man who didn't even know what Explo 72 was gave Bruce a ride. He laughed about it the next day. I wanted to cry.

Friday June 16th

By myself I rode around the city to further determine the mood of Explo 72. During the evening rallies, we had heard about the thousands of people who were 'giving their lives to Christ' around the city. I saw part of thousands who thought the whole scene was a bunch of crap. On a mall between Elm and Main Streets, in center city Dallas, the troops were in force with what was now the ubiquitous "Four Spiritual Laws." In some situations, one person was being "hit" by three people–from the front, and on either side. I watched one person who seemed to have a different group of delegates around him each time I would walk back through. He always appeared to be turned off by the whole thing, yet he never bothered to get up and leave during a period that was more than an hour.

Some were outright belligerent, and as I walked by I could hear the complaints or exhortations.

"Why don't you just leave us alone?"

"I believe it's good for you, but not for me, man."

"You got guts to do this."

"It doesn't make sense."

"You keep quoting the Bible, I don't believe in the Bible."

"I'd really like to believe this is true."

"Is it that simple?"

Finally, I decided to sit down and see how long it would take me to be "hit." Only three minutes passed before a girl meekly approached. Since I had been rather nice even when trying to be nasty, I decided to really test this person, and in this case it was the girl who inched her way closer, almost homing in like a bird that wants to be sure the territory is friendly.

"Have you heard of Explo?" she meekly asked.

"Have I heard of Explo! Who hasn't heard of Explo in this city?" I replied.

"Do you know what we're trying to do?"

"You're trying to convert people to your way of thinking, aren't you?"

The girl, Ivisa, who had come from Venezuela to live in America, did not reply so I tried to distract her by talking about Michigan, which her badge indicated she was from. Basic training had indicated that only under rare circumstances should they let themselves be dissuaded from talking about anything but the gospel. However, she was eager to talk about Michigan and was joined by another girl, also from Michigan. They talked about Michigan for about five minutes and then "zappo."

"Have you heard of this?" Ivisa said, pulling out an overused copy of the "Four Spiritual Laws."

"Are you kidding?" I said almost instinctively.

"Do you know the message they are trying to convey?"

"Look, I've had that book jammed down my throat all week. Why don't you tell me what you feel?"

In a move of gentle authority which shocked me, she put down the book and began telling why she felt Christ was the answer. It was so sincere and compassionate that I was choked up that this sixteen-year-old girl could have such feeling, such power, such wisdom. Actually, I hated to see it go to waste on me; but selfishly I wanted to hear, because in relation to Campus Crusade's approach as well as the approach of too many other evangelical Christian groups, Ivisa's message had a beauty that was worthy of modeling. No, I take that back. The message was beautifully effective because Ivisa was being Ivisa.

She explained how she had grown up in Venezuela and lived there until a little over a year ago. She now was struggling with the English language; but she was much better than she thought she was and her lapses into bad grammar only intensified my feeling that this was superior to the "Perfection" of The Four Spiritual Laws. She explained how "sinful" she had been living in Venezuela.
"What do you mean by sinful?" I asked.

"I would do bad things. I wouldn't love people who loved me."

One thing I knew for sure: this girl and the girl Betty sitting on the other side of me, loved me. I could feel it. The vibes were beautiful. I wanted to believe that these girls and the three guys, also from Michigan, who came up one by one, were typical of the high school and college students who were attending Explo 72; however, these were the ones who had the courage to share their faith and it was not guilt that motivated them, but the feeling they had something so wonderful that it would be tragic not to share it.

"Why should I buy your trip? I'm happy as I am. I don't need a new way of life," I stated.

"Trip?" Ivisa asked, not understanding the slang.

"He means why can't he just do things his way," Betty explained, showing an astute and quick sensitivity.

"I used to think I was happy," Ivisa said, "but with Jesus everything is so much better that I really believe no matter how happy you are now you could be happier with Jesus Christ. It makes me so happy and I would like to see you as happy as I am."

Reading this, one would say this poor girl either was on fire for the Lord or tremendously naïve; whatever labels people want to assign, seeing the expressions on her face and hearing the tone of her voice, I knew that this girl was for real. Physically, she was a beautiful creature; however, her attractiveness went far beyond the physical. Very frankly, I fell in love with this girl almost immediately because she was a diamond in the Campus Crusade for Christ's rough.

By the time she was finished, five people were surrounding me, each telling me about the joys of receiving Christ into one's life. Perhaps it was my basic male nature, but I seemed to respond more to the two girls. (It is interesting to note that Campus Crusade urges that men share with men and vice versa.) The other girl may not have considered herself beautiful by the standards we inflict on teenagers; however, she, too, was very beautiful. When her friend was in trouble with language or just didn't know how to respond to me, she came through with translations, insights, and most of all, love. For me, it was the high point of Explo 72.

When I finally told them that I was a Christian and a delegate at the convention, all five just stood and stared at me in amazement. Then, Ivisa jumped up and walked off in a mock Latin American temper tantrum that charmed the living hell out of me. But they all understood that this was the best way to get at the gut level of Explo 72, which contrary to all the shouting, grooving, and meeting, was in essence to train people how to share Christ and get on with it quickly.

*   *   *

Before the night meeting, I was told by members of The People's Christian Coalition that a reporter from the Washington Post had requested an interview with them. Earlier in the day, a delegation from the Coalition had gone to the "Reaching the Military for Christ" seminar and, because they were carrying signs that didn't exactly suggest that God blessed our military, they were asked to leave.

The women of the Coalition went to the "Women's Place in the Great Commission" seminar. There they were told, according to the girls, that men were really screwing up badly and thus the women had better get on the stick and work. Save the body – the Body of Christ, that is.

Earlier in the week, the higher ups from Campus Crusade had told The People's Christian Coalition that they could not give out some of the literature they had on display because Campus Crusade did not feel that it went along with the purposes of the convention. The Coalition protested (1) because they had been told that Explo 72 would be an open convention for Christian Groups, (2) many of the booths were outwardly or subtly supporting the military, (3) they felt their positions were in harmony with Scriptural principles and in no way contrary.

These officials decided to review the literature and came back the following day telling the Coalition which leaflets they could display and which they couldn't. The Coalition then gave Campus Crusade two options: they could call a press conference to announce that Explo 72 was not in fact an open convention, or The People's Christian Coalition would call the stated news conference. After contacting Bill Bright, they found that they thought it best to allow the Coalition to display all of their literature.

Since the coverage in the newspapers, more people were finding their way to the People's Christian Coalition booth.

A Chicano on the Crusade staff came to tell them that as a Chicano he found himself uncomfortable on the Campus Crusade staff and was going to resign from the organization. Steve, a second year seminary student from California, said that the People's Christian Coalition was the only breath of fresh air at Explo 72. The leader of another group like the People's Christian Coalition came up to find out if the group was Christ Centered, and after finding that to be the case, traded literature and urged that they keep in touch with each other, as well as trade more literature and ideas. A man came up to state that the whole group was being controlled by Satan. Earlier, Bill Bright's wife had talked to the girls of the Coalition, telling them that they were innocent girls who were being used. The ultimate was a gentleman who used scripture to try to prove his belief that the war in Viet Nam was indeed a Holy War ordained by God.

*　*　*

The stands in the Cotton Bowl were packed again as usual–only more so; for tonight, Billy Graham was to be the speaker. As in previous nights, two other places were showing the rally on closed circuit T.V. and anyone was free to attend…for a dollar.

The emcee and Bill Bright read excerpts from the two daily Dallas papers, which praised the convention, and the applause interrupted them often. Understandably, they failed to comment on the people who said the kids were naïve or pushy and the parents who complained about kids who either never showed up to the places where they were supposed to stay or showed up for one night. The following night they never showed up. They evidently wanted to spend the night with friends they had made and then neglected to tell their hosts.

One family said they had given up vacation plans in response to the urgent call for housing. They waited for two nights for the two high school students assigned to them to show up or call. They never showed up because they were re-routed to some unused apartment buildings that had not been completed. The following night neither the kids nor Campus Crusade took the trouble to inform the parents. Whether it was poetic justice or just rotten tragedy, an eighteen-year-old who lived in these unfinished apartments was raped and robbed by an intruder.

The emcee did express some grave concern to the delegates: everyone was buying bumper stickers, buttons, posters, pictures, etc. from the many Explo bookstores in the area, but very few people were buying the books and kits that they would need to continue their evangelism at home. Maybe they just weren't interested – after all it's just plain "groovy" to have some brother or sister honk in response to your "Honk if you Love Jesus" sticker; however, grass roots evangelism as well as social involvement and discipleship is tough stuff.

Billy Graham seemed intensely aware of this as he began his talk. He explained how when Jesus, James, Peter, and John went up into the mountain for the Trans- figuration, Peter suggested after this momentous event that they build three tabernacles in honor of Moses, Elijah, and Jesus, then stay up there for the rest of their lives. If anyone didn't get the subtle implications at first, he explained that the people at Explo were up on the mountain and that Christ wanted them down in the valley.

Continuing to talk about the intense cost of Christianity, Billy preached what I would have to consider not only his most intensely inspiring sermon, but perhaps the most moving speech by an evangelical Christian I had ever heard. Those of the People's Christian Coalition, who had by now adopted me, and who had leaned toward responding sarcastically to some of the things that went on in Explo 72, listened awe-struck as Billy pleaded with the people to realize that things were going to get hot for them when they left Explo and that many of them were going to "crash." He spoke in his intense, loud, and gesticulating manner, but this time it seemed to fit; his concern came through.

All great speeches have weak moments and this one's came when Billy leaned a little hard on the idea that being a missionary was the ultimate trip for the committed Christian. While he did mention that God needed Christian journalists, his inspiring stories centered around those who gave up everything and became missionaries, usually to some remote, Spartan part of the world. One such anecdote told of a rich man who gave up everything and went to the borders of Tibet. First, his two children died, and then while trying to get his wife to a doctor for help, she died; but before dying she told him to go back, which he did. Billy did have the decency to state that he wasn't able to authenticate the story.

After Billy asked anyone who was interested in committing themselves to the will of Jesus (at which 99 and forty-four sixtieths percent stood), Bill Bright instructed the people how to light the candles that had been passed out to them and urged the people to refrain from using flash bulbs so that the reverence of the event could be maintained. Two things happened to mar the event: (1) the wind was so gusty that probably less than half the candles remained lit, if lit at all; (2) flash bulbs went off in an obnoxious profusion during the whole service. As Bruce Bonecutter remarked:

"They claimed that we interfered with the reverence of their service when they had the military on stage and claimed that we didn't have Christian courtesy; yet these people ruin something as beautiful as this because they are more concerned for themselves than they are the welfare of others."

It was an excellent point. The Coalition had chanted for just about ten seconds and then stopped when the prayer began; however, as Bill Bright was praying that the Great Commission would be fulfilled in this generation, flash cubes were going off all over the stands in a manner that betrayed the lack of courtesy of too many people with too little concern. I personally felt they were more stupid than inconsiderate; for their miniscule efforts would yield nothing for themselves and completely ruin the pictures of people like myself who were smart enough to buy 400 ASA film.

* * *

The booth area was packed after the final Cotton Bowl rally. The once neglected People's Christian Coalition booth was now drawing the most attention. One attendant stood on a chair, head bowed, with his raised clenched fist holding a sign that read:

"TODAY AMERICAN BOMBS KILLED 300
PEOPLE WHO WILL NOT BE REACHED
IN THIS GENERATION"

[This was Jim Wallis who would go on to found the Sojourners magazine and publish a number of books including *On God's Side* and *The Great Awakening*. We were reunited for the first time in 2009 in Sarasota, Florida when I heard him lecture.]

The reference was to Bill Bright's statement that everyone would be reached for Christ in this generation.

Many stopped and looked in disgust, but the most disgusting thing was that few, very few, seemed to be impressed by the message. One man put it with terrifying succinctness:

"If you live in North Viet Nam, you're better off dead. The bombs are doing them a favor."

"It's a Godless country; they won't get to hear the claims of Christ anyway," another said.

What crushed me was that I heard only a couple of people in the five days I was there respond with anything that could be construed as love to the people who were on the communist side of the world, and it was even too rare that I saw love to the brothers of the People's Christian Coalition. If they are truly as screwed up as many felt they were, then more, in fact all, should have responded in love rather than the typical put down trip that keeps Christianity in the circus.

This circus atmosphere was best demonstrated right at the moment the booths were closing for the last time. A group of teenagers dressed in loud multi-colored coats and ties walked up to the booth and chanted:

> "EIGHT, SIX, FOUR, TWO,
> WE LOVE JESUS…
> DO YOU?"

They then pointed their fingers accusingly at the members of the People's Christian Coalition and glared at them as if they were the scourge of the earth. The incident filled me with both rage and nausea.

Driving back to the place where I was staying, the impact of Explo 72 was manifested on the radio. Two stations were simultaneously playing "My Sweet Lord" by George Harrison. I had heard bits of "Jesus Christ Super Star" all through the week. However, when the radio announcer stated that six theaters in Dallas were playing "The Cross and the Switchblade," I knew that old Dallas had been hit. Even during the news, the announcer stated that people were already making their way to the Woodall Expressway, which had been sectioned off to accommodate the expected 500,000 who would attend the massive Jesus festival tomorrow.

Saturday, June 17th

The supposed moment of modern Christendom had arrived – a Jesus festival where 250,000 to 300,000 would sit on their asses and praise God as well as be edified by the music of the Lord. Yes, this was to be the largest Christian music festival in the history of man. Leaders high in the Campus Crusade for Christ hierarchy claimed that the outpouring of Love demonstrated in this festival would be witnessed around the world. However, what happened (or, to put it more semantically correct, didn't happen) is manifestation of the long way Christianity must go before it is taken seriously by the majority of American people.

Many concession stands were selling posters showing masses of young people pointing their one way sign to the heavens under the title of "Godstock." What was happening, and what was to happen the rest of the day, didn't strike me as being very Godly and it certainly didn't come close to the feeling of community demonstrated at Woodstock.

The previous evening Billy Graham had warned the masses in the Cotton Bowl that groups of radicals were coming into Dallas to disrupt the festival and urged that the delegates push them back to where the policemen were (lovingly, of course) but not to forget to share "The Four Spiritual Laws." The fact that extremely few radicals showed up may point out that they saw what we didn't: that the festival would be a crashing bore.

Billy also said, "Some of this music you're going to hear might be a little different from what you would hear in church, but it does reach some people." The music I heard the eight hours of the festival was so super straight that I wondered who it would reach – other than those totally encamped in fundamentalist ways, those who wouldn't mind hearing the same old gospel music over and over again to the point of monotony. Many people I talked to, including died-in-the-wool fundamentalists, couldn't believe how dull the whole thing was.

I remember at Woodstock a feeling of communion and an element of the human and the humane. The announcements of lost people, appreciation for the Army's sending helicopters to evacuate the sick, and the humor of the announcements in general were in blatant contrast to the announcements at this festival:

"Randy Barton….your bus is leaving in fifteen minutes and we've been told to tell you that they're going back to New Jersey without you if you aren't on that bus when it leaves."

"I want to urge you not to accept any free drinks if they are offered to you. Don't take it…it could have acid in it." (Campus Crusade for Christ was getting 35% of the concession and whether the two were related, I honestly don't know.)

"Whoever owns a light blue Pontiac [I couldn't hear this part] or it will be towed away."

Since I owned a light blue Pontiac and had parked close to a freeway entrance, I decided that I had better check on it. Arriving at the area where the announcement was made, I asked policemen and Campus Crusade people to help me in my predicament; however, they demonstrated what I have seen too much among people in full-time Christian work: an attitude that reeks of "Bug off, I'm busy doing the Lord's work." This attitude was capped by one of the Campus Crusade Staffers walking into the crowd in a rather uptight manner: "Give me a pen, I need a pen." I pulled out my $2.50 pen and handed it to him, asking him where he would be. [$2.50 was expensive for a pen in 1972, and it was only pen I had.]

"Don't worry about it, you'll get it back," he snarled and walked off.

I never saw him or my pen again. I sarcastically comforted myself with the reality that the pen was lost doing the work of the Lord.

I couldn't get any of the Campus Crusade people to help me, but finally one of the policemen took pity on me and walked to the stage area asking if someone of the staffers could help me locate my lost pen He must have had no luck or just given up himself because I waited another half hour in vain for him. Another policeman told me that this was the most disorganized event that he ever had to work.

Using the Quaker influence of my non-evangelical days, I figured that emotion spent over my lost pen and perhaps my towed away car would be wasted emotion and thus went back to experience the festival. As I walked back to an area where I could see, Kris Kristopherson was telling the crowd that he hadn't been to church in thirty years and I inwardly cheered this non-typical and refreshing comment. He was there because Johnny Cash asked him to come.

This musical session and the songs that Larry Norman sang were the only departure from the mundane. Everyone else had been wallowing in sin until Jesus came along and, hell, I think this is a beautiful reality; but I'm getting tired of seeing someone as beautiful as Jesus getting riddled to death with mundane and predictable clichés that haven't changed since I was a "teeny-bopper Bible banger." Even Johnny Cash jumped up on the "tell 'em what they want to hear" bandwagon.

For the whole period from seven until three in the afternoon, malaise and boredom pervaded the festival. The crowd was way short of the original estimation. Campus Crusade claimed that the crowd was nearly 200,000; however, the Dallas police estimated somewhere between 80,000 and 120,000. As I looked around, I didn't see many people who didn't have the Explo 72 delegate badge on, and some still had their little white wrist bands dutifully clinging to their wrists.

Perhaps because each performer felt that this was going to be one of the biggest events in Christian history, he didn't feel the motivation to do anything. Yet I still found it hard to understand how over 100,000 people, most of them in their teens, could be so lethargic after nearly tearing down the Cotton Bowl in the name of Jesus.

Naturally all the performers sang about Jesus, and while this might fringe on blasphemy to some, eight hours straight of hearing songs about Jesus (under a hot sun with poor sound to boot) is a bit much. Even if the temperature were fifteen degrees cooler and the sound of Woodstock quality, things wouldn't have been much better, as the lyrics were trite and the music mundane. It was Brahms' "Variation on a theme of Haydn" with lyrics hinting that Jesus is the only way to go that really irked me. I have little problem with the theology. However, the repetition led me to wonder whether they were trying to convince themselves as well as the "unsaved."

Larry Norman rose above the monotony and because of this I got the idea that a lot of the teenagers really didn't know how to take him: he was the only counter-culture oriented Christian in the whole festival, except maybe Kris Kristopherson. His opening song poo-pooed the idea that rock music was Satanic:

"But why should the devil have all the good music," he sang in the chorus. In Mobile California this might have been more appreciated; but this was staid Dallas and all it got was a few appreciative snickers and that was it. Larry Norman is called by some the thinking man's Jesus freak, and he might have been too much for the crowd here.

"They just carried a fourteen year old boy out on a stretcher," the emcee stated. "They think it might be from an overdose of drugs. Like I said, don't accept any free drinks."

I've never taken acid or any other hallucinogenic drugs, but the temptation, if they had been available, would have been great.

"We really want to thank the Dallas police who have done a terrific job," the emcee continued. "Let's have a hand for the Dallas police."

Despite the fact that the Dallas police got almost as much applause as Jesus, the effort appeared miniscule in relation to the applause of the counterculture people at Woodstock when the announcer mentioned that "those men you call pigs have come from the Army bases to help those who are sick." Perhaps it isn't fair to compare, but I compare simply because I expect more from myself and other people who dare to call themselves Christians. At least no one was shouting "pig." In fact, few people were shouting anything.

Not even the arrival of Johnny Cash aroused much excitement. He was the star attraction…except for Jesus, of course. Like the rest of the day, the group arose from their lethargy only when something super-evangelistic was belched out to fit their computer card mentality. If it didn't fit in the hole, it just didn't get any response despite talent revealed or honesty portrayed.

Finally, Billy Graham spoke and uttered the most uninspiring and banal message I had ever heard, complete with literal interpretation of how Adam and Eve screwed it up for us all in the Garden of Eden. Even the loyal must have been bored because when Billy asked the masses to chant "God Loves you," it came out like they had to get up off the john to say it. Not even T.V. engineering and editing could make it look enthusiastic. When Billy finally gave the invocation, a paltry few stood up.

That was the festival and I walked out in disappointed disbelief at how this event fell so short of what it could have been. Weeks later, I asked my wife, who was not with me at Explo 72, to watch the three special programs, the last of which was highlights of this Jesus festival. I figured that editing could make it look better than it was; however, editing didn't help at all; and they left out Larry Norman and Kris Kristopherson. After forty-five minutes, my wife claimed that she had seen enough and walked off. In mock legalistic fashion, I dragged her back into the room and twisted her head toward the T.V. as Bill Bright was assuring the audience that this was one of the greatest events in the History of Christianity. She screamed trying to block out the sound and squinched her eyes closed despite my joyous pseudo-legalistic efforts to pry them open.

"You're gonna burn in hell if you don't watch that," I said.

"How did you stand it?"

" I stood it because I don't want to wallow in the flames for eternity, and you had better repent fast, Sister; otherwise you is gonna miss the heavenly boat."

"If that's where the heavenly boat is going, you can count me out."

We rolled on the floor with laughter as I continued to force her head in the direction of the T.V. and our laughter intensified as Bill Bright pointed out that the joy and love were certainly evident. Just what did ol' Bill see that I missed? I laughed about it then, but from the standpoint of Christian witness it really isn't that funny. That day could have been so great and a positive witness to all aspects of Christianity; but it turned into a sterile fiasco.

Well, at least no one – except the one who was raped and robbed – was hurt; and my car didn't get towed away after all.

Addendum

It is now 2015 and 53 years have passed since Explo 72. At that time I had stayed with Rick and Carol Monk in Texas. With Rick I had many fond memories from the two of us singing in a folk group called The Lakesiders. I took Rick with me for all the sessions and took Carol with me the night The People's Christian groups chanted "stop the war!" I am sad to report that Rick died a year after Explo 72 of a massive heart attack at age 35. Attempts to locate his wife Carol were futile.

I don't know if Bill Bright is still alive, but Billy Graham is still with us and his son, Franklin, is condemning people of the same sex who wish to get married.

Ivisa will be approaching age 70, and I have no idea where she is or whether she retains the zeal and fervor that she had at age 16.

I have had no luck contacting Bruce Bonecutter.

I personally have come a long way since my evangelical Christian days of 1972. I guess you might say I have "fallen away" or been taken over by Satan. I by choice am an agnostic, who chooses to write about the wrath of God and the terrible things He did to us humans. You can get all of these books (listed in the back) through The Book Tree in San Diego, California – the contact info is on or in this book should you be interested.

9

From the Circus to the Arena

A Vision for the Return to Real Christianity

There's a darkness upon me that's flooded with light.
In the fine print they tell us what's wrong and what's right.
And it comes in black and it comes in white.
And I'm frightened by those who don't see it.
–The Avett Brothers

In the late fifties, my alma mater Dickinson College was not blessed with an effective football team. Thus, those who would normally use a touchdown as the excuse to pull out the flask and take a swig formed what was called the First Down Club. Things got so bad that during my sophomore year, the "club" settled on the gain of five yards or the completion of a pass as sufficiently satisfying. At one game, our team's efforts were so paltry that only two such occasions manifested themselves during the first half. After a particularly dry period of more than twenty-five minutes, it began snowing. Three rows in front of me, a desperate student stood up and chanted, "It's snowing…drink!"

This anecdote could easily be compared to the state of Christianity today. We have become so "flabby" as Christians that we have had to lower our standards in order to rejoice at efforts which would have been miniscule to the early Christians.

A few years ago, His magazine printed a story about fruit pickers who would allow one of their people to pick a peach. Then all of them would stop work to sing joyously about the victory in picking that peach. This rare piece of satire was not even hinting at social involvement, but made fun of the pathetic state of Christian evangelism. The Christian circus seems to have gone the way of educational circus: if the organization cannot get its constituents to rise to the established standards, then for heaven's sake lower the standards. Otherwise people won't be motivated to join. In education this is bad enough. However, Christianity is a faith that can function only on total commitment, and any bastardization of Christ's original intentions leads Christianity to the farce that it is now.

To call Christianity a farce will upset many. Nonetheless we have perpetuated the farce by refusing to admit that we are accepting the farcical as Christianity. I have worked with collegiate Christians who by their tunnel vision would tell you that the Campus Christian Groups are making a dent for Christ on the campus In reality, more than ninety percent on that particular campus have never even heard of the Christian groups. Such naivety and willingness to see the miniature as magnificent is destroying Christianity and turning it into a self-edifying "ego trip."

Some liberally oriented Christians appear more willing to listen to the need for internal change than their conservatively oriented counterparts. Yet I find neither really willing to embrace the effort and pain which it will take to bring Christianity back to its original force. Ironically enough, I find that the evangelical Christians might be this force that will blend the spiritual and the social and return Christianity to its revolutionary status. This may reveal tremendous bias; however, any radical change within Christianity will come only from a Christ-centered impetus around the belief that Christ is Lord and letting that reality impact them. Many evangelical Christians are already there. If they can give up their self-edifying ego trip of drooling over their salvation and embrace the powerful social aspect of discipleship, they will become a revolutionary force.

However, it could happen the other way around. In Sweden, the liberally oriented state church youth have embraced and demanded a spiritual commitment to Christ, yet have retained their concern for social issues. Sweden is already showing some signs of marching toward the arena. Where it begins, I really don't care, but I want it to happen soon.

For Christianity to be really effective, we're going to have to dump some of our sacred cows. We can begin by tearing ourselves away from the idea that America is a Christian nation founded on Christian principles. In fact, we might begin facing the reality that Christianity has sold out to American principles. The ideas of America's free enterprise society do not correspond with the American Christianity by coincidence. Instead, American Christianity has been the chameleon willing to change its ideals when things "got a little hot" or when social and national advancement were imminent. We just might be at that point when being a good Christian might mean being a bad American.

For example, Iraq is a touchy issue, yet what we are doing in the name of stopping Islamic radicalism is one of the most ungodly acts in history. To equate dying in a war, which few people really understand, with the martyrs of Christian history is an insanity from which one day I hope we as Christians will understand – and not only be able to divorce from the Christian experience, but also accept it for what it is: rendering unto Caesar that which is his. Perhaps someday we might even be able to rise above the all-encompassing interpretation of that little verse.

What is really sad is the manner in which Christianity has embraced the American cultural ethic. We try to increase our membership in relation to quantity rather than quality. It's almost as if the church has decided to build its Christians in the same manner that Detroit builds cars; get as many as possible without any real concern about how long they last. [Things have changed significantly in this area. Cars now do last longer.]

Therefore, one part of a blueprint for sane Christianity would be to separate American values from Christianity. Whether America is a great country or not is not really the issue. Christianity should be a powerful faith and can make it on its own ideals without selling out to the American way of life. The Bible advocates loyalty to the government; however, this loyalty does not necessarily condone bearing arms for that government; especially if that government goes contrary to the principles of Christianity.

If Christians were really following the precepts of Christ, they would be making it hot for America and its leaders instead of kowtowing to the government in an "I don't wanna rock the boat, Massa" attitude. If Christians did respond in this manner, America would be a better country, and Christianity would be a credible faith.

Another part of this blueprint would be for Christianity to get off the quantitative numbers trip and move toward making Christianity a quality faith. For Christianity to be a quality faith, it would have to dump its three-ring-circus approach and let its people know that the only place for Christians to be is in the arena of life. As essential as it is for Christians to move in this direction, it's just not that easy. We have conditioned ourselves to escaping the world's problems instead of embracing them. We have conditioned ourselves to seek success in numbers that look good before a church board rather than accept a Christ-like discipleship, which rarely can be measured on paper. No matter how hard the transition, we must return Christianity to the priority of Christ's words rather than the priorities of church boards and Christians who find the total commission of Christ getting in the way of what they consider Christian.

We must stop bringing Christians into the fold as our top priority because: (1) it really hasn't done a thing for Christianity from the standpoint of its impact on American society; (2) by selling out to recruitment, we have deadened the original thrust of Christianity ("And we will know they are Christians by their love," etc.) We can concentrate the few who are willing to carry Christian action beyond church attendance, Bible study, and youth groups and those who practice it seven days a week instead of one. Even if we lost ninety percent of those who call themselves Christians, we would still have such a revolutionary force here in America that would supersede all the ersatz revolutions that never got beyond the dreaming boards – our first revolution would appear inferior in contrast.

History has shown that the numbers of the Christian body grow when Christians decide that they are going to live according to the gospel of Jesus rather than the gospel of convenient Christianity. It happened in the early church; it happened somewhat in Nineteenth Century America; it can happen now. Ministers who suggest that their congregations cease worrying about church membership and start working on the quality of the church may find themselves doing a lot of traveling from church to church. In their travels, they might come upon that church that has a committed core of people who want to serve rather than be served. The church that turns itself away from doing those things that make people want to come to the church in the first place (good preaching, good cheer, good youth programs, good buildings, good social events, etc.). It does those things that Christ taught (social involvement, loving your neighbor, evangelical effort, personal discipleship, etc.) is going to lose people. There's no way to avoid it. However, those who leave will be no loss; we will have simply trimmed the fat and left the meat.

Yes, the minister will have to look at empty pews. People will say, "what has happened to that wonderful ol'Pastor Crawford; his sermons used to be so comforting; now he wants us to ruin ourselves by looking inside ourselves instead of outside for Christian growth." When I mentioned to a fellow leader that our Young Life club should begin getting involved in some social service projects, he urged me to "cool it" for a while; he feared that we would lose up to two-thirds of our members by doing such a thing. I "copped out" by compromising and thus held the membership of our club firm...for w while. We also held the sterility and ineffectiveness of the club firm. When I brought an ex-convict to talk about how these kids could help out in the prison, the membership did drop and it dropped further when I mentioned opportunities for work at a children's home.

The more liberally-oriented Christians have another type of problem. When someone suggests that they be more spiritual in their approach, the response is cold. Churches that display efforts in the area of social involvement find that they can go only so far without the spiritual aspect of Christianity. When they finally have leadership that suggests this course, people have flocked to other churches much in the same manner that conservative Christians run away when leadership decides it's time to get involved in social issues. This dichotomy will always keep the numbers high in the Christian circus. We have become a computer card faith: just about anyone can find a church where he can do his thing and stagnate under the illusion that he is furthering the kingdom of Christ.

Still one can sometimes see sparks of commitment beginning to glow in the arena. Churches and cell groups alike are realizing that discipleship is both spiritual and social. Instead of getting "hung up" on labels like "fundamentalist" and "humanist," they just get down to the business of Christian commitment. They know where the arena is, and they know that God can help them there. They have risen above conservatively and liberally oriented Christianity and thus have drawn criticism from both sides. The potential of what they can do is exciting to those who are waiting for Christianity to rise above its cultural ties to America. This is devastating to those who like the comfort of that "ol'time religion" or the pseudo stimulation of the "right-on, super relevant" religion that changes with each full moon.

These arena people are rare, yet they, because they know their mission and the source of their power, are the hope of Christianity's re-establishment. They first of all take seriously the greatest commandment of Christ. Thus loving their neighbor is not some love-just-your-Christian-Brother "cop-out." These Christians bring drunks home to sleep off their stupor and then offer shelter and food until they can get back on their feet. They don't just leave it to the Salvation Army or just pray for that person as he walks by. Others visit the prisons or hasten the recovery of mental patients by their presence, their concern, and their love. Even then their love doesn't stop, for they are willing to be friends to those people when they are released.

These "arena centered" Christians are going where many of the so-called committed Christians fear to tread. Some are working with emotionally disturbed and autistic children sometimes they are bitten, scratched, and unappreciated, but they know that temporal rewards – while humanly desired – are futile. When one measures the love involved in these actions to the once a year effort of a youth group to go caroling at an old people's home, one can understand how much the concept of Christian social service has deteriorated over the past years.

The real problem that has inflicted Christianity over the past fifty years has been the conservative Christian's escape from social involvement. While this behavior emanates from a genuine concern that social involvement might be practiced at the expense of the spiritual, it has gone so far that even Christian young people now quote Christ's statement that we'll always have the poor with us – to justify a "sit-on-your-ass" Christianity.

Conservative Christians have deluded themselves into believing almost totally in evangelism despite the irony that very few of these Christians really wish to get involved in evangelism. Those courageous enough to participate in evangelical efforts seem content to experience the narcissistic joy of "winning a soul for Christ" (another notch on the spiritual gun) Few display a commitment to remain and help that "new born soul" grow either as a person or a Christian disciple. Part of the reason for this problem lies in the fact that those doing the "converting" have little Christian growth to share. Many of them come hot off the conversion experience themselves. This situation reeks of the inexperience leading naively with conservative Christianity suffering from high numbers of people high on idealism but very short on depth and commitment. While the conservative Christians might be winning the numbers game, they are far short in relation to their credibility among the "non-believers" and very short on discipleship.

How conservative Christians ever allowed themselves to be conned into thinking that Bible studies, cliquish fellowship groups, church attendance, and prayer groups constituted the bulk of discipleship is one of the great mysteries of modern Christianity. If the above-mentioned efforts were used as a spring board into the arena, that would be a different story. However, these efforts are more often circus-oriented escapes from any commitment to walk into the arena. I have wanted to sit down and cry sometimes about how high school Christians have been brainwashed into believing that they are fulfilling their Christian commitment by doing only the paltry expectations of their conservative leaders or parents. This is a "suck the nipple" type of Christianity. As hard as its going to be, we had better start the weaning process soon.

The more liberally oriented Christians have other problems. To begin with, the label "liberal" is somewhat facetious; I have too often found the liberal Christians as close-minded as the fundamentalists they malign (or at least ignore). Where the fundamentalists "cop out" on the social commitment of the gospel, the liberals "cop out" on the spiritual commitment.

So many of my liberal Christian friends can escape discipleship by not taking the New Testament seriously. Many find it inspirational, but are almost embarrassed to even consider that these words might be the inspired words of God (no matter what man did to them in the course of history). Others find Jesus much easier to relate to as a gifted teacher…but not the Son of God. In matters of a relationship with God, the idea of a loving and concerned God is squelched to the safety of sterility. Because of this mentality, the more liberally oriented Christian, just like the conservative Christian, can pick and choose his form of Christianity from scattered fragments of Scripture.

The liberal Christian may be more involved in social discipleship; however, this effort while impressive in comparison to the near do-nothingness of the conservative Christian churches is paltry in comparison to what is being done by only a few model churches. The commitment to love your neighbor and love without condition is painful. It is difficult no matter what camp the Christian identifies with, and the lack of commitment and a refusal to embrace discipleship are evident on both sides of the Christian fence.

One might ask, surely some churches exist that embrace the best of both sides? But actually, few do. The fact that few churches of this type exist reveals the tragic polarity in Christianity. Christ's disciples held divergent viewpoints; however, He succeeded in keeping them oriented to the kingdom of God as a priority. The early Christian managed to do this; however, differences began dividing them, but never to the point of the inert mediocrity that Christianity reflects today. A Christianity that embraced a commitment to both the spiritual and the social would be revolutionary by today's standards. Yet we must have that revolutionary Christianity, not only for the sake of our withered faith, but also for the sake of our country.

The early church did not need emotional conversion experiences, pseudo-relevant facades, or "groovy" times to win people to Christianity. People came because something was different in Christians' lives. Today we have people who show no difference whatsoever stand up and try to tell people that something is different in their (the Christians') lives. Many of the early Christians were not afraid to pay the price of discipleship. Because of their actions they were persecuted. Today, we call it persecution if someone calls us a do-gooder or a Bible beater. The early Christians told those who listened that the cost would be high, and they grew both in numbers and spirit; we sell Christianity as a neat faith with little cost and are surprised at our shrinking numbers and dying spirit. We live in a time when the leader who comes closest to advocating the total Christ is considered the most radical. The one who plays the weather vane to either the conservative or liberal wind is considered the greatest among his followers. It's a bad age.

I have often wondered what would happen to Christianity in America if Christianity "found" itself and had the courage to face all opposition in returning to the principles of its founder. These thoughts have often crystallized into a vision and this vision haunts me. Often I lapse into spasms of reality. This happens especially when I have tried to convert my dreams into reality with the Christian work I did as well as my circus attitude preceding, during, and after my study for the ministry. Despite the fact that the increasing apathy in American culture has also pervaded American Christianity and the fact that we have been retreating deeper into the Christian circus, I refuse to abandon the dream – because anything can happen in this age of rapid change. For the effectiveness of the Kingdom of Christ, something good must happen.

*   *   *

Diary of a Christian Revolution

Nov. 5th: Two friends approach me one day claiming that like the five blind men and the elephant, we have only seen a part of Christianity. They frankly admit the emptiness that comes from depending more on the goodness of man and realize that perhaps God is a living power, perhaps even a personal power. I admit that pursuing salvation alone is a truncated form of Christianity and that involvement in social issues is a part of the gospel. We set up a time to have more organized dialogue.

Nov. 9th: We are now six, and because we refuse to adhere to the liberal or conservative poles in Christianity, we are few and feel alone. On a one-to-one basis, a discontented evangelical Baptist begins talking to a discontented liberal. Both are surprised how small their differences really are. At first, the Baptist complains of the uptight legalism among his Christian friends. This seems to block rather than enhance his Christian growth. The Epicopalean is tired of picnics, church membership drives, spiritually dry sermons, and yearns for a never experienced spiritual growth. We first criticize, laugh, and eventually weep over what has happened to Christ's vision for His church. We agree to meet again.

Nov. 16th: Next meeting we each bring a couple of equally concerned friends. We find that being astute in recognizing problems is easier than coming up with solutions. We decide to pray for guidance and meet again next week.

Nov 23rd: We talk about ideas we have had the last week. One mentions how he read that old people are being abandoned at hospitals. He asks if we could comb our churches for people willing to take care of these cast-out people. One of the conservative Christians asks if some of the people in the liberal Epicopalean church would be interested in a Bible study on discipleship. However, this one would differ in one major way: the students would be asked to put in practice what they learned as well as share both success and failure with the others. We agree to try it.

Dec 10th: Our group is only ten; however, the quality of the impact has manifested itself. A plea for help for the abandoned old people in both churches is slow at first. A widow in her sixties from the Baptist church volunteers to take two of the less sick women from the hospital. A bachelor in his seventies agrees to take one of the men for a while. Three of our conservative members organize a Bible study at the Epicopalean church. The minister is concerned, but realizes that many have a hunger to learn about the Bible that evidently his academic sessions didn't fill. Many are impressed with the conservative layman's knowledge of the Bible. The conservative laymen find the views expressed by the liberals refreshing. What they didn't find is major and incapacitating differences of opinion. These differences center more around doctrine and dogma than what can be found in the scripture. What amazes us is that when we try to be doers of the word instead of hearers, the results are beautiful. We put into practice the admonition of John to resolve conflicts with our brothers. Old grudges begin to dissolve and friendships flourish.

Feb 8th: Our group is now twenty-three. A Catholic priest calls and asks if he can sit in on the next session. Also visiting this session is a "down-and-outer" who had been invited home to dinner and given a place to stay by one of the group's members. He and the priest listen with interest as we discuss our successes and failures as Christian disciples. We don't have to put on anymore; we rise and fall together. The down-and-outer gives us workable information about how Alcoholics Anonymous helped him. He also mentions how the offer of food and shelter kept him from going "down under" again.

The rest of the meeting we spend in organizing an effort in both churches to help others with the same problem. Father Reed promises to bring the idea up to his parishioners. As the skid row man listens, he finally asks, "Can Christ really make that much of a difference in a person's life?" After the meeting, both liberal and conservatively oriented members share why they believe.

Feb 15th: Father Reed brings six of his parishioners plus another priest. Enthusiasm is high as we talk about helping the people on skid row. We Protestants realize our in-bred prejudice as we see that the Catholics really are not that concerned whether they join a Roman Catholic church, a Protestant church, or any church, for that matter. A couple of the Catholic members and one of the conservative Protestant members are Pentecostal. However, they all agree to center their priority on service and allow God to delegate gifts. Some of the evangelical people want to begin "witnessing" right away but realize they are witnessing already by responding in love.

Feb 22nd: We try to find homes for some of the skid row people. One of the members has gone to all the missions to make sure that there is no animosity or conflict. We find only joy at our interest. All missions offer to help as well as suggest people who could benefit the most. On Sunday, one of us will speak briefly at each of the represented churches in our group, asking for help in this area.

Feb 24th: After the service only one or two from each church respond to the weekly call to embrace Christian discipleship. Some ask for a guarantee that these people be clean or that they not use any foul language. Later in the day, a couple more call: one because she realized it was futile to call herself a Christian if she couldn't love "those people" at a point more than just from a distance. Another family volunteers because their two children urged them to do it. Still the number of homes offered is far short of the need.

Mar 1st: My minister declares from the pulpit that he will open his home to one of the needy because. He explains that the Lord led him to the conviction that he couldn't be a spiritual leader if he himself could not respond with love. In a Methodist church, one of the women who responded walks uninvited up to the pulpit and berates the people for their lack of response. The head minister surprises everyone by thanking her and reiterates what she said. A few get up and walk out. The rest remain silent. In the Catholic church, the plea is made once again, with a couple more families responding positively...and a few walking out.

Mar 4th: One of the fraternity houses at the local college produces the invitation to have three of the needy come fill their empty beds. Three from that fraternity ask if they can come to our meetings. None of them had attended any Christian function for a long time because they had become disillusioned, but this group gives them the hope that Christianity really could be "alive."

Mar 7th: Two mainline drug addicts come to our meeting, and the words they speak are painful because they don't even know how they can be helped except to describe how hopelessly hooked they are. All three are helped by methadone, but they speak emphatically of how they really want to get at the source of the problem. One gently asks if she would be willing to consider the possibility that Christ could help her with her problem and their response is positive. Slowly many are beginning to get that Christian discipleship centers more around action than inaction.

Mar 14th: We get together for "rap sessions" with each of the "mainliners." One says, "I can conquer it with Christ." he then tells us how he wants to help others with his problem, and we ask him how we can help. He asks if we'll "guide" him through a cold turkey.

Mar 16th-18th: This cold turkey takes three days. More than twenty members of the group make sure that at least three people are with him all the time. The experience is horrifying yet eye-opening. Not one of us could have guessed the pain and agony that a mainlining drug addict experiences during withdrawal. We also needed time to recover. But we have an intense motivation to do anything to insure that a person would not get on hard drugs in the first place.

Mar 21st: We start to realize that there are no real clear-cut answers to the mainlining drug problem, but agree to keep pursuing the matter. Almost unanimously, all of us express a concern that church attendance is dropping significantly since laymen, ministers and priests had urged social involvement as part of Christian commitment. We realize that the pressure is high on the ministers to not only bring those people back but also to avoid saying anything upsetting that would only drive more people away. The group asks those ministers and priests attending if they are willing to keep supporting the program. The Epicopalean minister admits that he would be "copping out" if he didn't continue the program, but he is also afraid that he will be asked to resign and sincerely wonders how much good he would be to the effort if he had to move to another town. The Baptist minister claims that he had been trained to preach the gospel and that's what he still wants to do; however, he frankly admits that Christians must live the gospel. The two priests are somewhat concerned, but they know that they have it somewhat easier because they have no family commitments.

Mar 23rd: The four spiritual leaders get together in one of their homes to pray about and discuss the matter. After four hours of "soul-wrangling" and agonizing, they firmly agree to participate in and support the effort as well as urge their people to get involved. They intend to publicly announce this to their congregations Sunday.

Mar 26th: The "rebellion" is now open. Many openly threaten to leave and/or cut off their financial support. At the Epicopalean church, the addict who committed his life to Christ stands before the congregation and states that the drug problem is only a symptom of a spiritual sickness in our land. Many squirm uncomfortably, yet some listen with hunger. At the Catholic church, some complain about the mass being interrupted for social opportunities announcements; others feel that the mighty Catholic church has lost its soul; however, still others offer praise and encouragement. They feel that the church is experiencing the new Pentecost that the late Pope John had envisioned. The Baptist church is the hardest hit, as people after the service reiterate that the pastor's job is to preach the gospel and to leave the social issues alone. However, the pastor calmly yet firmly states that more have made commitments to Christ. They also expressed an interest in Christ as a spiritual basis for their lives in the last three months – outside of their church than during the last three years within their church.

Mar 28th: Fewer than half the people now attend the Baptist church; however, I feel almost a gut level sense of commitment among the members who remain. I find it harder to "cop-out" and rationalize my desire to return to the circus. At the Episcopalean church, about two-thirds remain, but there is still fear that things are going to fall apart. The minister, a little shook himself, stands up before the congregation and states with a shaky yet committed voice that he would rather have himself and his church sell out to Christ than to the wishes of the people. At the Catholic Church, Father Reed states emphatically that a new reformation for both Catholic and Protestant is needed and that both Catholic and Protestant must make it happen.

Apr 2nd: About forty people, fifteen of them being a youth minister from a Lutheran church and members of his youth fellowship, had called and asked if they could visit. The core of twenty-five people is no longer enough for the tasks that they've got to do. People have been calling up asking for help with a number of problems. During the meeting they collect money, food (and other items) to help a black man who had switched jobs and wouldn't have been able to switch to the better paying job unless someone had lent him the money to get by till his first pay check. The one helped also explains the need of two of his "soul brothers" who need financial help. They need help getting their repossessed cars back until they could get jobs again. The ministers and priests present promise to take a special offering the following Sunday and search out other financial means. We decide to place the following ad in the local paper:

> IF YOU ARE HURTING, WHETHER IT
> BE FINANCIALLY, SPIRITUALLY
> OR SOCIALLY, WE WANT TO HELP.
> IF YOU ARE NOT TOO PROUD TO
> RECEIVE HELP, WE ARE NOT TOO
> APATHETIC TO TRY TO HELP.
> CALL 385-8361 ANYTIME

Apr 10th: No one expects the number of calls from people young and old who want to help. Some offer experience in drug counseling; others offer to organize and spearhead efforts to collect food, clothes, and money to supplement charity organizations' efforts. The youth group that had attended the previous week wants to open a coffee house where people could come and relax, rap, talk about problems, or talk about God if they wanted to. They agree to get the support from their own church.

Apr 17th: We realize the need for organization as we see the impossibility of our task. We also realize the danger of over-organization as well as the need for prayer that is action centered. We agree not to form any type of new church. We have no real desire for publicity except for when people need help, then they will know where to go. Christ and His commissions is one priority.

Apr 24th: Another group of five or six people come and ask us if it's all right to organize another non-competitive group in the adjoining town. We are not only overjoyed with the idea, but offer to work with them until they can get rolling on their own.

May 15th: The second group is going strong and is actually taking some of the heavy burden off us. Like our group, they are not divided by the fact that some speak in the tongues of the Holy Spirit and others claim the need for social justice with a rather strong tongue. They somehow seem to realize that the vision of Christ is complex and demanding enough to provide a place for all.

May 22nd: A visitor from another state visits one of the meetings and is so excited that he wants to try the same thing back in his town. Three of the more mobile of us offer to go with him claiming all they need is room and board. The man offers his home, and another potential mission spreads.

Oct 3rd: Eight to ten groups are now in operation. The quality of their Christian fruit is a beautiful witness. I recollect with shock the standards of Christian discipleship I had before. We go to churches and ask them to give homes to rehabilitated prisoners. We volunteer our services at local mental institutions and prisons…we open eyes, hearts, and pantries to the hungry… we participate in or lead groups for those who wish to grow spiritually. Prayer groups are no longer people who pray and vegetate, but people who pray with at least some motivation for being part of the solution. Bible studies are no longer just self-edifying academic exercises, but sessions that search for precedent and inspiration to make the Christian role of discipleship an act that affects more than just the disciple.

Dec 14th: About fifty groups are in full swing or despite the concern that having many groups would cause a fad-type situation. Because of this, we give groups that ask for guidelines exactly that and nothing more. As each individual group grows, so do the threats to the churches. We are called middle-of-the-roaders because we refuse to buy the polarity of their former doctrines. We are ironically called radical by both conservatives and liberals because they go much further than either…not to mention deeper. Liberals tell us that we will "plunge American Christianity back to the 'idiocy' of the revivalist period.'" Conservatives tell us that the group is "abandoning the blood of Christ in the name of social action." "Christ-centered" people picket our meetings because they feel that we are not spending enough time winning people to Christ. The reality is that people in our group are winning people to Christ because they are practicing Christian discipleship rather than simply talking it. The so-called "un-evangelized" are asking questions without the need of a Billy Graham Crusade, the four spiritual laws, or even the coffee house ministries that many people from our groups have set up on their own. Christ is a potential reality to these searching. The reason is that the Christian people who are reaching out are finally real. We want to work through the churches and make personal pleas for help in our projects. This, to put it mildly, is making many people uncomfortable. We face the painful reality that any church that agrees to allow their members to ask for involvement to the point of more than just a cursory announcement is experiencing a drop in attendance and membership. The hardest hit churches are those where ministers, priests, and members are taking a stand.

Dec 21st: The mass media have caught on to us, and we a try to decide whether this is a blessing or a hindrance. They do point out our diverse spectrum, ranging from devout Catholics to disenchanted Baptists to staunchly liberal Episcopalians. Since the media must have rousing labels and metaphors, Chris Matthews refers to the groups as "The Arena Christians" and compares us to the early Christians. We are honored but realize that we have quite a distance to cover to be worthy of that allusion. However, the persecution does build. More and more we realize that "Love your enemies" means just that. We begin plans to help the war-torn people of both Bosnia and Kosovo others had way before us. We include the countries of the Communist enemies, some ribs and skulls are broken: Christians who believe Caesar is unjust in asking them to participate in hate and destruction of the enemy, become an "active " threat. Some of us get in trouble because we personally complain about oppressed and exploited tenants of the ghetto and organize legal action for them. Sometimes we pay out of our own pocket, and this upsets many, but strangely enough not those who are giving the money. A friend of mine is beaten and told to "let Christianity return to the church and allow the government to take care of the poor people." One of the lawyers in our group defends an Indian's right to receive better compensation for land, which was taken from his grandfather. He is not only politely asked to leave his prestigious Athletic Club, but also told by his pastor that he "might be happier in another church." Persecution builds and we fear a turning point in the movement.

Dec 31st: Turning point it is. History has shown that persecution is a sure way to make a movement grow, because it strengthens the resolve of the committed and discourages the potential quitters. Loss of life is realistically considered gain and Jesus' words are now something more than cute aphorisms which titillate. Letters of inquiry come from not only every state now...even from other countries. An iron curtain country ambassador publicly states, "This type of religion is definitely not the opiate of those people." T.V. officials are frustrated because they feel they can't visually capture the essence of the movement. Few people hold hands to the sky or chant effective epigrams; instead, they just quietly get down to the business of loving people and Christian discipleship. Yet somehow the people are getting the message. "By their fruits shall ye know them." Love, compassion and the joy of service come across without all the external pundits. A new year comes tomorrow. I'm both excited and scared – it's getting hot.

*   *   *

If such a vision became reality, the average person in the United States would realize that no matter what his problem, people who call themselves Christians would try to help or find someone that could. People would see that most evangelism doesn't necessarily happen in the revival tent or church, or on a giant Crusade. The genuine evangelists, like Billy Graham, would eagerly wait to "be put out of business." Where the social and spiritual were so polar, people now would wonder how they ever got separated in the first place.

Christians would once again get into the mentality that their faith is a doing faith rather than a talking faith. As happened in the Middle Ages, some would be slandered; others threatened; many are criticized and urged to "return to Jesus", the faith, or the fold. Other "Christians" would claim the new movement is inspired by Satan, although this time their claims would be countered with the New Testament words of Christ.

Some would insist on comparing this movement to the short-lived Jesus movement. However, this movement would not be a trip; it would be a journey. A Christian would begin to look upon his commitment to serve as an opportunity rather than a demand, a joy rather than a bother, and the means to help oneself by helping others, rather than just having the best experiences for herself.

Those who refer to Christianity as a comfort trip will still be in the majority. However, the core that have decided to be doers rather than hearers of the word will grow gradually in both spirit and number, and churches will change from within. Because of the witness of these arena-centered Christians, people will begin more and more to accept the reality that perhaps Christ does make a difference, that perhaps He really is alive after all, perhaps being a Christian really isn't just for the pious, plain and poor in spirit. As the word acid changed in the new context of the drug movement, the word church will take on its original meaning because of the new Christians.

People will begin turning their cheeks instead of just preaching it. The term "salt of the earth" will become more than just a metaphor. Widows will find that they are no longer lonely.

Prisons will become crowded with visitors. The term social action will gradually fade into the Christian discipleship. The peace that passeth all understanding will no longer be interpreted as the absence of conflict. Naked people will be clothed instead of ostracized. Hungry people will be fed instead of just prayed for. The Church of Satan for the first time will get a little scared.

Ministers will be thrown in jail because their Christian beliefs conflict with those of society.

Spiritually thirsty people will be quenched with love rather than pamphlets. More Christians will refuse to kill no matter what the cause. Love will become a deed rather than just an inspiration.

Inertness will establish itself as a higher sin. Faith and works will begin to blend. Healing will happen from people who love other people. Christianity and freedom will no longer be antonyms. Christian children will become Christian men and women. "Losing one's life" will no longer be considered a loss. The scattered sparks of Christian effort will begin to blend into the light of the world.

Many Christians will begin to look redeemed.

Some will actually give more than ten percent to the church, or charity. The cries of the poor will finally be heard. Reborn souls will not wither. Money will be lent without concern of repayment. Justice will be given to the weak. The needy will be rescued. The confused will be listened to. Oppression will be both shared and alleviated wherever possible.

The afflicted will be comforted.

The comforted will be afflicted.

Lip service will be transformed into service. The word "Christian" will once again have a cutting edge.

Jesus will be free once again because his sheep have stopped being sheepish and have decided to commit themselves to the Lamb of God.

* * *

Things were tough a while back. A man named Peter stood in a town square a few days after he had denied his best friend; yet he firmly told the people that this friend of his was the answer.

"Come on, Peter. You're gonna get the Sanhedrin all upset and ruin it for the rest of us."

"The law says move on, buddy." It'll never work, Peter. It's too radical."

Another named James walks within moments of death from an angry sword, claiming that the new way can change lives.

"James, you keep talking like that, you're going to get hurt."

"What are you getting so uptight about, fella?"

"Why can't you be a good Jew just like the rest of us?"

"Look at him lying there in a pool of blood. Now tell me, just what did he accomplish?"

A boy barely out of his teens named John, who was known to be one of the favorites of the radical rabbi, is no longer timid. His authority in voice and commitment to his risen master create a dichotomy of thought.

"Hey, John! You gotta lot of guts, but don't you think you're overdoing it just a bit?"

"Come on, kid, wait till you get a little dry behind the ears; then you might begin to accomplish something."

"If you got it made so good, then why are you bothering to go to the synagogue?"

"You cure me, little punk. I haven't walked for thirty-eight years. What makes you think it's going to be any different today? Just give me some coin and move on."

And a strictly Orthodox Jew who insists that this radical rabbi talked to him while he was journeying to Damascus changes his name from Saul to Paul and changes a few other things in the process.

"Ol'Rome is going to get you, Paul. Then where will you be?"

"Are you stupid enough to think that you can pick up that snake and live?"

"Things must really be bad if you can only get teens like Timothy and a few freaky women. You gotta have quality if you're going to change things."

"Let well enough alone, friend. I'm happy just where I'm at."

"Nobody's ever got out of this jail."

"Weren't you the one who held Stephen's clothes when he was killed? And you want to tell me that you've changed?"

"What makes you an authority on what changes are needed?" Which university did you come from? A few years from now, people won't even know your name."

Previously a radical rabbi named Jesus marched to his death while some cried. Others breathed a sigh of relief.

"Thank God they are getting rid of this guy. He almost ruined our faith for good. He broke the law and should be punished."

"Did you see how his disciples scattered? We'll never see them again."

"I'll just be glad when that Jesus is safe in his grave."

*   *   *

In Jerusalem, I stood on the spot reported to be the grave of Jesus. A sense of grief struck me and I prayed the following prayer: "Jesus, I have no doubt that you came out of this grave. What I wonder is whether your church can rise above the crap that we have insisted on calling Christianity. I can't help feeling that the task is going to be harder than moving the stone."

I had just completed seminary and was fulfilling my lifetime dream of spending some time in the Holy Land. Standing on top of a hill in the barren desert between Jerusalem and Jericho, I marveled that a world-shaking faith germinated while the Son of God and twelve men walked in hot sand and God-forsaken hills. But eleven of those twelve, plus others, went out to the world and rattled the foundation of established society.

APPENDIX A

Jakov Speaks on the Divine Imperative for Lust

Due to the interest of Jakov expressed by some in previous Bible study meetings, we present the following appearance, by popular demand. It may not have a direct bearing on Biblical scripture, but covers ethical and sexual issues that are often frowned upon by the more devout in the faith.

Greetings, brothers and sisters in the light. I channel to you today through Galiana who has offered herself to me so that these divine words could come to you and that the light of truth might shine through. Today, my words of truth might be a little tough to swallow, but let me remind you that most great truths that are accepted now were at one time considered false or even blasphemous. Such, I am sure, will be the impact of my words today.

So often the consensus reality of a planet has come to embrace absurdities that have later turned out to be false. Consider how long you persisted in the belief that the world was flat. Then Columbus went forth in his three boats and proved that was wrong. Did Columbus fall off the end of the world as so many predicted? I say unto you that he didn't, that he actually proved that the world was round and eventually proved that he didn't know squat about how to adminster over a colony of natives whom he felt should be brought over to the Mother Church forthwith.

Yet, just as people laughed at Columbus and called him a blaspheming heretic before we went out and proved his point, so will you here gathered today be tempted to do the same. I encourage you to withhold from participating in such immature exhortations and keep an open mind for a truth that has been ignored for thousands of years.

It is divinely ordered by God that men should pursue and enjoy hard bodies. By hard bodies I mean young girls in their twenties. It is in no way evil to lust after these divine and innocent nymphets; these angelic creatures have been put on this planet to be enjoyed. Now for those of you from America who deign to think that I might be just a tad politically incorrect, I wish to make one thing perfectly clear: old men have been placed here for the enjoyment –

not to mention education – of young women. I have absolutely no intention of being sexist about such sacred matters. God said to go forth and multiply, so us old farts need a final chance to pass along our genes. We must continue the species as God intended.

I am a male spirit who has had the good sense never to come out in a female body, so I shall thus proceed from the perspective from which I am most comfortable. Very few are going to know the divine promulgations of the channel Sergei Jakov, the first divine channel to emerge from a remote part of Russia. As the tensions vanished between the United States and the old Soviet Union, we have found an openness to ideas from other cultures, no matter how strange they might appear.

[Galiana's body suddenly jerked uncontrollably and a new and wildly strange voice came through.]

I'm sorry but I have to interrupt here. This is Punani, a divine etheric spirit from the American sector. I just can't let this psychotic drivel continue. This etheric Jakov's main problem is indeed that he has never had a lifetime as a woman, and therefore knows nothing of that which he is talking.

Piss off, Punani, you disembodied wench. This is my session.

You are a sick etheric shit who has managed to be disgustingly sexist no matter what dimension you inhabit.

Come on, Punani, you're wearing out the channel. She can't handle both of us. Besides, what I have to say is of ultimate spiritual concern to humanity. Listen to me. Older men have always had these lustings for teen-age girls (those of legal age of course), and you have considered this sick and sinful. I am here to tell you that those wonderful feelings that you have are of divine origin. This is God saying, "Listen humanity, if I didn't want you lusting after younger women, I would have made them ugly until they were at least thirty years old."

I just can't let this go on. You are mocking the Lord, claiming that He created young girls for pleasure, that He created these young girls simply to be sexual objects for a group of dirty old men who can't make it with women their own age.

Well, what's wrong with that? This is what the Lord hath ordained. Everybody wins. The young women are initiated into the divine experience of wisdom and sexual union with older men. Wait a minute, I see someone is getting up and leaving. Sir, I am the mighty Jakov. I am able to transcend time and space and am thus able to read thoughts and perceive dreams. Should you insist on proceeding any further to the exit, I shall be forced to reveal to this crowd of 300 what fantasy you were indulging in when you were masturbating last night. And I must assure this audience of seekers of the light that this fantasy did not have any older women in it.

[Pause. The man moves back to his seat.]

I knew you'd see things my way. As I was saying, the church has done men a great disservice by making men feel guilt about this divine longing they have for teen-aged women. Of course, society has backed this up by frowning on this divine pursuit. This means that this divine longing can only be fulfilled with women our own age whose breasts sag almost to the floor and look like dried grapes and asses that droop so they can hardly walk and...

I must stop this sickness now!! You are truly an evil etheric spirit.

Punani, I'm getting damn tired of your spouting this anti-divine and anti-lust diatribe. Good God, lady, in your last life you entered a convent when you were 14 years old. You had this firm butt and luscious breasts, and were worthy of prolonged bouts of oral sex, and what did you do: you hid all of this light under a bushel... well, actually a habit. This is what I'm trying to say: partake in the gifts of the Lord. As it says in the Song of Solomon, "When the fruit is ripe, then shall ye eat it."

Jakov, you are confusing the leadings of thy etheric penis for the divine longings of the soul.

How would you know? Confess, foul woman, that thou sufferest from etheric penis envy. Wait a minute, I see that a man and his wife are getting up to leave. Are you two going to force me into telling this audience what you two do in the darkness of your bedroom? I mean it. Stop right now! I know that you think using enemas is a natural part of sex, but I.... Hey, that's better. I knew you'd see it my way. If you had gotten out the door I would have been forced to tell this crowd what you are doing with the neighbors. Well, enough of this. It's time now for some questions from the audience.

Question: Do you see any problem at all with eighteen-year-old girls?

The only problem I see with them is that they eventually get old like me.

Question: I'm one of these teen-aged girls you're talking about and I think that everything you have said is disgusting. The last thing I want to do is have sex with a dirty old man.

Don't knock it till you try it, honey.

Question: Don't you think that old women should have the pleasure of eighteen-year-old boys?

No way! That would be perverted and disgusting. Let's not talk about this. I see that Galiana, the woman who channels me, is losing dangerous amounts of spiritual energy and, for her sake, I will end the session now.

ALSO BY JACK BARRANGER

Past Shock: The Origin of Religion and Its Impact on the Human Soul. Mankind is out of balance today because of visits from ancient gods, what they did to us and much more that is revealed in this book. Vol. 1 of the *Past Shock* series. $12.95

The Origin of Religion and Its Impact on the Human Soul. How and why the ancient gods programmed a "slave chip" into mankind and why it is still with us today. Vol. 2 of *Past Shock*. $15.95

Freedom from Religion. Reveals how to break free from our ancient programming. You will want your freedom even more if you read this revealing book. Vol. 3 of *Past Shock*. $14.95

When the Gods Return. If aliens do land and reveal themselves, they will not be cute and cuddly! What to do when they come back. Vol. 4 of *Past Shock*. $12.95

Rico's Irreverent Bible Studies: Fifteen Outrageous Lessons You Never Learned in Sunday School. by Rico T. Scimassas (aka Jack Barranger). $13.95

Knowing When To Quit. How to tell if your job or relationship is at a dead end and what options you may have. One of the best selling self-help books of the 1990's, now available again. Jack's first book, a standard self-help work which made him hugely popular. $18.95

Mysteries Explored: The Search for Human Origins, UFOs, and Religious Beginnings, by Jack Barranger and Paul Tice. Two authors tackle the biggest mysteries they could find and come up with startling conclusions. $12.95

www.ingramcontent.com/pod-product-compliance
Lightning Source LLC
LaVergne TN
LVHW051656080426
835511LV00017B/2601